MW00718878

Sentenced
to Hospital!

abdul o odemuyiwa M.D.

ISBN: 0-615-44565-9
ISBN-13: 978-0-615-44565-6
LCCN:2011901997

ABOUT THE AUTHOR

Educated at King's College, Lagos, Nigeria, Dr. Abdul Odemuyiwa attended medical school at the Lagos University Teaching Hospital and thereafter obtained a postgraduate degree in toxicology from the University of Surrey, Great Britain. He became a board-certified internist after successfully completing his residency program at Wayne State University, Detroit, Michigan.

With experience as a hospitalist, an emergency room physician, and an independent medical examiner, Dr. Odemuyiwa—fondly called Dr. Ode by most of his patients and colleagues—has a versatile experience of over twenty-five years in medical practice across continents—about fifteen years in the US—and has been chairman of the Department of Medicine at Henry Medical Center, Stockbridge, Georgia; is the current chairman of the Medical Executive Committee of Southern Crescent Hospital for Specialty Care Riverdale Georgia; is a medical director of both a hospice and a home health care company.

Dr. Ode is also certified in wound care as well as hyperbaric oxygen therapy; he is a board-certified internal medicine physician and also board-certified in hospice and palliative medicine. He has carried out peer reviews for insurance companies and workers compensation boards, and he has worked in a state psychiatric hospital providing medical clearance and support for psychiatric patients. He presently runs a medical and weight loss clinic in Stockbridge, Georgia, and actively admits patients in three local hospitals. He has taken care of thousands of patients both within and outside a hospital setting. He is a civil surgeon for the United States government and performs physicals for immigrants to the USA. He has in the past evaluated patients for Social Security disability benefits and also serves as an expert witness.

Dr. Ode is the treasurer of the Association of Nigerian Physicians in the Americas, Georgia chapter. He comes from a pedigree of medical practitioners. His father practiced medicine for several decades, and his mother is a retired midwife. His brother is a cardiologist practicing in the United Kingdom and his uncle is an endocrinologist in the New York area. His interests include traveling, meeting people, and volunteering his time to the needy. His most important duty is continuing to be a loving husband to his wife and a role model to his daughters, who remind him daily of the privilege of being a parent.

ACKNOWLEDGEMENT

First and foremost, I would like to thank the Creator of the universe and the giver and taker of life for the good health that most of us enjoy. Next, my brother-in-law, Attorney Temi, whose constant but subtle pressure ensured I completed this book over the three years it took to write it.

I thank my childhood friend of over forty years, Ayo, who always had something encouraging to say. I am grateful to Genie Trafford for her excellent contribution on nursing homes and also for proof reading this book. I thank Professor Kasim Alli for his very constructive criticism of the manuscript. I also acknowledge my friends, too numerous to mention, for having a listening ear at various stages of writing this book.

Finally and in no way least, I thank the love of my life, my wife, my best friend, F.S.T.; and my kids, Toni and Tobi, for the lack of attention they endured while I was writing this book that never seemed to end! I promise to make it up to you somehow, someday very soon.

DEDICATION

This book is dedicated to "the patient," a term almost everyone will be referred to at some point in their lifetime.

TABLE OF CONTENTS

INTRODUCTION

Every new car comes with an owner's manual, a book the owner can refer to on how to operate the car and all the gadgets the car comes with. Along with the owner's manual comes the service handbook. This tells us when the first oil change should be, as well as the recommended service depending on the mileage of the car; it also includes the timing for tire rotations, checking the tire pressure, and so forth. As the car ages, more and more has to be done in order to get your money's worth in the form of optimal performance.

A lot of people know off the top of their heads what needs to be done to their cars at various stages during ownership, but ask these same people when they need a colonoscopy, or better still, what a colonoscopy is, and you draw a blank stare. The most common defense is that they have never had any health problems; therefore why go looking for a problem when they are in seemingly good health? My response is that when you take your car in for an oil change, does it already have a problem? We usually do not wait until the car develops a problem before we take it in; we do a lot of preventive maintenance on our cars, so why not on our bodies? Surely not all preventive maintenance on our cars or our bodies will prevent all future problems, but they will certainly go a long way toward preventing catastrophic outcomes in future.

Being stuck with a vehicle problem on a lonely highway at night with no help in sight is the equivalent in my mind of a human being having a stroke. In some cases the car has been giving some warning signs, which have been ignored by the owner. We seldom have any warning signs from our bodies; we therefore have to make a conscious effort to look for them. Even when we do find and address the warning signs, some problems still occur. When this happens, at least we have the inner peace that we did our best to try to avoid undesirable outcomes. When one has suffered a stroke or any other medical complication as a result of neglect it is often too late to turn back the hands of the clock. The individual ends up being sentenced to hospital in an attempt to make them whole again.

This metaphor can carry over into just about any other area of life. We plan for our financial future, but not for our medical future. We make plans for our career paths, but not our bodies' health. Just as there are numerous books written on various financial and real estate topics in the marketplace, we need more information from medical experts in easy to understand language for the general public to refer to. Most people use nonmedical family members or neighbors to help them diagnose their medical conditions simply because these people have had the same symptoms in the remote past! What a lot of people don't know is that medicine is a very complex science that is evolving on a daily basis. The same symptoms in two individuals are most likely due to different problems. Even a recurring symptom in the same individual may be due to two very different causes, and in most cases it requires a medical professional to carefully differentiate them.

This book is a humble attempt to provide all adults with the medical life manual we need as we attain adulthood and also dispel a lot of the myths acquired from nonmedical relatives and neighbors. I will also point out the most common errors patients make and how to avoid them. Just as following a car manual is guaranteed to increase the lifespan of your car, using the information in this book is guaranteed to prolong your life, or that of a relative or loved one; however, it is a gross oversimplification of medicine and should never be used in the place of professional advice from a qualified physician. I am convinced that by reading this book the life of at least one person will be saved, and thus the book will have achieved its objective.

This book addresses most of the errors I have experienced patients making over the twenty-five years I have practiced medicine. I address both common medical problems of the inpatient (hospital, rehabilitation center, long-term acute care hospitals, hospices, and nursing homes) and outpatient (office) settings.

CHAPTER 1

How to Choose an Internist or Primary Care Physician

An internist is a physician who specializes in *adult* medicine, just like a pediatrician specializes in the care of kids till they are young adults. The internist takes over until the client is sixty-five or older, and then geriatricians may take over care of the patient. An internist is *not* a medical intern, or a physician who has just completed medical school and is still under training, which in the medical world is the lowest rung of the ladder.

Everybody should have an internist, also called a primary care physician, who knows about their medical history in detail. The internist also knows about most medical topics and is able to recommend tests or procedures to the sub-specialists. In some small towns where there is a shortage of subspecialists, some internists end up performing some procedures that are usually carried out by subspecialists; for instance, you may find an internist doing all of the colonoscopies as well as the stress tests in a rural hospital setting.

One of the first things you as a patient need to know is if your internal medicine doctor is board certified. This can usually be done through your insurance company or through the American Board of Internal Medicine's Web site. The next thing you want to know is if your doctor goes to the hospital or not. A doctor who does not go to the hospital is not less qualified than those who do; however, a lot of my patients defected to my medical practice because their previous physicians did not go to the hospitals even though they were excellent doctors. This is an individual preference; some people prefer to be taken care of in hospital by their own doctor, while others do not really mind as long as they have a good doctor caring for them.

It is very important to have your primary care physician within your locale, as well as to have as many of your physicians as possible within a reasonable distance from where you live. Even if you have a complicated medical history that is being handled by a tertiary health care institution, it is in your favor to have local physicians who know your case very well because in the event of an emergency the ambulance will most likely take you to the nearest emergency room. In the United Kingdom, patients are given a choice of practitioners within their neighborhood, which makes a lot of sense and would also save a lot of health care dollars by eliminating unnecessary duplication of tests.

How do you choose a PCP if you have no clue and no one has been assigned to you by the insurance company? The first step is family and friends in the neighborhood. This is the only time that I approve you seek advice and a recommendation from nonmedical professionals. The other way is to call or take a trip to the nearest emergency room. Ask for the charge nurse or look for a nurse with a very friendly face and ask him or her to give you the names of three primary care doctors in the community. Another way is to call the hospital referral line; most hospitals have a physician referral line these days. The referral line operator will give you a few names based on your criteria. The most convenient way is to go online to the physician referral line of the hospital and find some names yourself. I suggest you always have three names to choose from. Next, call the offices of the physicians recommended and see if you are impressed with the office staff and their phone etiquette. When you choose from an insurance booklet you do not get a feel for a physician; you are blind as to the physician's personality, work style, work ethics, practice style, and friendliness of the staff.

One of the questions I always ask my patients is how they chose me as their physician. The first reason overwhelmingly is by friends and family recommendations. The second is through hospital referral, and the third is by insurance company assignment. When I ask those who picked me randomly from their insurance booklet why they chose me, most of them tell me my name intrigued them! All I tell them is that I cannot believe that something as serious as choosing a physician is decided on by a name! Some tell me that my staff were very polite and kind over the phone and did not seem to be in a rush. Others tell me the fact that they were able to talk to a live person was good enough for them! Some tell me that my staff revealed to them I am very well loved by a lot of my patients and that once people sign up with us they hardly leave. In most cases the standard of care and the kind of treatment you will receive from different primary care physicians is similar. It is those other little things that count.

In my career I have had only three patients walk into my office to "interview" me for the job of being their primary care physician. When I asked them why they came personally, they all used the same word: *chemistry*. They came to find out if we could get along well with each other. They are all still my patients and have referred several other patients to me over the years. On the other hand, when I see some patients for the first time I can tell that we are not going to get along well together. At the end of the visit I usually advise them to find another physician before we got too deep into the relationship. Remember certain "blind dates" you have had in the past? The ones you could not wait to end? You knew right from the beginning you would not want to see that person again even if you were paid to!

There are also a lot of cultural factors involved in choosing a physician. Some patients like doctors from a certain part of the world because of their bedside manner, while some people feel others from another part of the world are too arrogant! Please do not fall prey to these generalizations because they hardly hold true. As for me, I am the blunt guy! I always call a spade a spade; I do not mince words. Some people resent this while others welcome it. If you do not want to be told the truth, stay away from our clinic!

The First Visit with the New Primary Care Physician

You have put in a lot of effort in finding a new primary care physician. This is progress! For your first visit, I suggest you go with a family member, neighbor, or friend who can be your health advocate. I definitely recommend all patients over the age of sixty-five to be accompanied by a family member, preferably a younger member of the family, in addition to their spouse.

Be sure your new doctor has all your medical information, such as your laboratory data, X-rays and results of any procedures done in the past, especially the abnormal ones that need a follow-up. Try as much as possible to get your records to your new physician prior to your arrival. You also need to take with you *all* your medications or write them down as accurately as you can. Ensure that the list includes the medication, dosage, and frequency as well as the number of refills left. Also, be sure you have enough time and patience for the first visit since your insurance has to be verified; this can be done electronically in most cases and by phone in other cases. Finally, you get to see your new doctor. It will help if you have a list of complaints or issues you want to discuss with him or her. Be clear and to the point.

Your new physician will go through a process called "taking the history" to review your chief complaint and the circumstances surrounding it. The physician will ask you questions like when you first noticed the problem, the frequency, duration, and aggravating and ameliorating factors. Please answer all questions as truthfully as you can in order to assist in eliminating possible causes of your complaint.

Next your physician will go through the past history of all your previous illnesses and hospitalizations in brief, as well as the surgeries and outcomes. It is okay to mention procedures as well; your doctor will decide how important the information is in relevance to what your complaints are. Regarding surgeries, *all* previous ones need to be mentioned, not just recent or major surgeries. For instance, if your main complaint is abdominal pain and you have had your gall bladder and appendix removed, this completely eliminates these two as sources of the current problem. I cannot tell you how many times physicians have ordered an ultrasound looking for a gall bladder problem and the results come back indicating the gall bladder had been surgically removed! This is a waste of time for the physician and a waste of money for the patient, who will end up being charged for this unnecessary test.

Your doctor also wants to know the medications you are on, the dosages, and the frequency of administration. This is extremely important, and medications have two names, the trade name and the pharmaceutical name. Whichever name of the medicine is easier for you to remember is the one you should know. Let us take Ibuprofen, which is marketed as Motrin, a very popular brand name in the US. It is also the active ingredient in Advil, Anacin, Arthrofen, Brufen, and Calprofen, to mention a few. Just stick to whichever name is easiest for you to remember and pronounce.

Also inform your physician about any herbal extracts or vitamins you are taking from the health food store. They are very popular these days, and there are side effects to some of them when taken in excess; for example, there's a report linking excessive consumption of green tea to kidney stones. I always ask my patients to bring in all their medications at every visit. Medication reconciliation is an integral part of the primary care visit; I can also easily estimate a patient's compliance by checking the medications. Some of my patients tell me the medications are already in my records, and I give them a simple analogy. Why do most people keep a check register and not rely on the bank to monitor and keep track of the checks they write and the balances? What if the bank makes a mistake? It is always beneficial to the patient and the physician to reconcile medications they are on; it serves as a good means of checks and balances. I recently prescribed a diabetic medication for a patient who was dispensed a blood thinner instead by her pharmacy, and I was only able to discover this by reconciling her medications. This particular patient was semiliterate and had a reading challenge! The pharmacist's excuse was the age old one…they could not read my writing!

Many people have no idea what they are taking and why. In this case the physician's office staff has to stop what they are doing and try and find the patient's pharmacy number so as to get the medication list from the pharmacy. Some patients, of course, do not have the pharmacy phone number; they only have a physical description of the pharmacy! Some do not even know what pharmacy chain they patronize. Most people tell me they are taking a little white pill for blood pressure and a small yellow pill for cholesterol, the pink one for cholesterol and the little blue pill for erectile dysfunction! This is useless information to most physicians, who hardly see the medications they prescribe; even a pharmacist will find it challenging to decode the information by color.

Next, your primary care physician will ask you about your allergies. A lot of patients list adverse reactions as allergies; a lot of people including me have an adverse reaction to aspirin, but God forbid if I am having a heart attack I would definitely take an aspirin because of the beneficial effects! A true allergy involves a reaction to the medication in question that could be life threatening. A certain type of patient always has a long list of pain medication allergies; physicians feel that a lot of these people are drug seekers. They try to arm twist the physician into prescribing what gives them the buzz by claiming they are "allergic" to viable alternative pain medications. Your physician might question you more about these so-called allergies. Some people say they are allergic to metronidazole, marketed as Flagyl. It causes a metallic taste in the mouth and also has an anti-abuse kind of reaction, meaning that if you take the medication with alcohol you are almost guaranteed to vomit your guts out! A colleague of mine found that out the hard way in medical school. He does not have an allergy to metronidazole; he just made a bad choice!

I have a personal story of an allergic reaction. As a

young physician I was exposed to a suspected rabies case and was advised to get a rabies vaccine, which I did. While driving home I suddenly felt my lips were heavy and I started itching all over. I then noticed that people were staring at me while I was driving home. I took a look at myself in my rearview mirror and could not recognize myself; my lips were almost the size of my face! Needless to say I had a true allergic reaction to the horse serum used for the rabies vaccine in those days.

Next your physician will want to know your occupational history, habits, and in some cases your sexual orientation. Patients usually get very upset when physicians ask about this touchy subject. We are not trying to judge you; most of us never do, we just need the information in order to eliminate certain illnesses that occur most commonly in people of a certain sexual orientation. I had a female patient of mine land in the emergency room once very sick, and I consulted my infectious disease colleague, who indicated that she was well known to him and is HIV positive! This patient had never told me she was HIV positive during the several years I looked after her; when I confronted her, she said she did not believe that she was HIV positive. Again, be as truthful as possible; if you have been previously diagnosed with a certain medical condition and have your doubts, just say so and ask for a second opinion. Never pretend you do not have a disease; in most people this behavior is denial, and we in the medical community are aware of it and are ready to assist you in coming to terms with your diagnosis. Let your doctor know that you do not believe the diagnosis, and he or she will be happy to rerun tests to prove or dispel the diagnosis in question. I have seen a lot of people hold on to valuable information that would hasten a diagnostic process and probably save their lives. The information you give to your physician is confidential, and your physician will protect it; rest assured you will not be made fun of, judged, or chastised for that one-night stand that gave you a sexually transmitted disease.

We also want to know where you work and what you do at work and if you drink or smoke now or ever did. I remember the story of a young man I admitted for alcohol-related problems. This was documented all over his chart from the emergency room through admission onto discharge. I got a call from his wife days after discharge asking me to change his diagnosis to a non-alcohol-related problem in order to save his job. He apparently had signed up for a job that had a zero tolerance for alcohol abuse and dependence, and they were asking him to sign a release authorizing his employers to obtain his records from the hospital. I felt sorry for his wife and family but informed her that it is against the law to alter medical records; the only defense he had in my mind was to refuse to sign the release. Either way he was sure to lose his job.

This brings me to another point about medical records. Most patients erroneously think medical records are with the physician who takes care of them. This is not true; the records are usually at the *place* of service, so if you were cared for at a hospital, the records are with that hospital, and if the care took place at a physician's office then the records will be at that office.

Last but not the least, we want to know your family history. What kind of medical problems run in the family? What kinds of cancer have members of your family died from? What other problems have family members died from? There are many instances of public figures dying from illnesses that run in their family. Not long ago a television personality died of colon cancer, and later the news media indicated that his mother had also died of colon cancer. With this type of family history, the offspring deserve increased surveillance and colon cancer screenings as recommended by their primary care physician based on the specifics of the case. Similarly, a very well-loved producer of a talk radio personality in Georgia recently died suddenly in his home at the age of forty-three. According to media reports he had earlier told his wife he was not feeling well and then suddenly collapsed and died. An autopsy later revealed he died of a massive heart attack. The talk radio host he worked for later revealed on the same show that his father had also died in his forties while waiting for a heart transplant! This to any physician is a red flag that indicates a patient should be screened for coronary artery disease and other heart ailments at an early age. The only excuse for not knowing your family history is if you were adopted.

This is the general outline of most of the information an internist or primary care physician would want from a patient. Other specialties or situations may demand a more detailed history of a patient's lifestyle. For instance, a travel history may be pertinent if your physician suspects you have an ailment that is rare in your home country. I saw a gentleman once who was admitted through the emergency room with fever, chills, muscle aches and pains, and some other symptoms that made me suspect he had malaria. The only other thing I needed was some confirmation of a recent history of travel to a malaria-endemic area. When questioned about any recent travel, the gentleman got very irate. "I feel lousy and all you can ask is if I have traveled recently! Well, if it is important to you I just returned from a short trip to Ghana with a friend of mine." I asked him if he had taken any prophylaxis for malaria. It was then that the light bulb went off in his head! He had malaria, confirmed by a blood smear; he had developed almost every complication in the book, including kidney failure, and had to be dialyzed a few times. He was able to recover fully but spent a very long time in the hospital. Sometimes that is the entire clue needed to clinch a diagnosis.

An allergist may want to know about pets or contact with animals. I hope you get the drift; sometimes not all the history is obtained during the first visit, or rather some patients do not tell it all to their physicians. Then during future visits they reveal an important health problem they failed to mention earlier. To get the best out of your physician, I advise that nothing be held back at any encounter. From my experience the most important medical information is obtained from patients just as I am about to exit the examination room. "Doc, by the way…"

The next step in the diagnostic process is the physical examination. This can vary from specialty to specialty, and it also depends on your complaints. At the minimum your physician will examine the anatomical area you have a problem with. He or she may extend the examination to other areas you may think do not have anything to do with your complaint. For example, if you are diabetic your doctor may decide to look into your eyes or examine your feet, looking for signs of complications of diabetes or just looking for signs to confirm what may be wrong with you. If your physician decides to carry out a more detailed body examination and you are of the opposite sex, he or she will have a chaperone who is present to protect both of you. At the end of the examination the physician will have a list of possibilities in mind—what we call differential diagnoses— and then in general will proceed to order investigations to confirm or discard the differential diagnoses by a process of elimination. The tests that are ordered are generally non-invasive to begin with. I am sure most people would not go back to any physician who plans to operate after the first visit! A negative test result sometimes provides more information than a positive one. For example, if you suffer from headaches and your physician carries out an MRI, which is negative, at least it's evident that you do not have a brain tumor! Some patients regard this as a waste of money, and also an indication that a physician does not know what he or she is doing. Please stick with your physician until you get to the bottom of your complaints; do not change doctors in the middle of the diagnostic process if you can help it, and if you do be sure to take the records of all the tests you have done to your new physician, or you might find yourself repeating the same investigations, which can be very expensive to you even with insurance. Your physician will usually give you medications to treat your symptoms while he or she tries to find out what is wrong. It is at this point that you do not want to discuss your symptoms or investigations with your neighbor!

Diagnosis

How does your doctor know what is wrong with you? I agree that we have made tremendous strides in the world of medicine. Regardless of the advances made, physicians still need a sort of "history" of the illness or what is wrong with the patient. Unlike cars, where diagnostics can be run and immediately tell you what is wrong with the car, human beings are a bit more complicated. In some very few and select cases, by talking over the phone or asking a few questions, a doctor can diagnose simple problems like an upper respiratory tract infection or an uncomplicated simple lower urinary tract infection. In other cases it is not that simple, even after several days or weeks of investigations.

I was on call one night at a local hospital and was asked to see a patient who had been brought in by his sisters from a nursing home in Florida. He was young and bedridden and apparently had been estranged from these two sisters for a long time; another sister who was this young man's primary caregiver resided in Florida, and the sisters who brought him to hospital didn't know anything about his medical history. I introduced myself, asking what was wrong with their brother. This was their response: "You tell us, after all you're the doctor." I knew I was in for a long night. I tried calling the sister in Florida, but she would not answer her phone. This was about one a.m. early Saturday morning, I called the nursing home the patient had recently been discharged from only to be told his records were in the medical records department and could only be accessed during working hours. One nurse could, however, tell me he had suffered a stroke. This was somewhat obvious, but why would such a young man have a stroke? I proceeded to order some basic tests and reviewed the CT scan of the brain already done. This confirmed a stroke, and I proceeded to admit him into the hospital. I later found out that the patient only needed placement, and even though he had suffered a stroke because of substance abuse he also had some in-herited blood disorders that made him more susceptible to stroke. He was later placed in a nursing home after about a week in hospital.

Your physician needs information on you. We do not have a magic wand that tells us what is wrong. The more information we have, the better and more quickly we can help you. Sometimes the speed by which we obtain infor-mation can be lifesaving. A better way to have handled the situation I described above was to have obtained cop-ies of the patient's medical records from Florida; this would include his X-rays and CT scans and the latest blood work. It would eliminate the need to repeat these tests, saving a lot of time as well as taxpayers a lot of money. The only other way to obtain this sort of information is if all hospitals and nursing homes in the country have some electronic medical record system that can be accessed by other facilities twenty-four hours a day, seven days a week. I do not see this happening because of the expense involved.

So the process of arriving at a diagnosis, as stated above, begins with a history. Your physician wants to know a lot about you. Please make an effort to provide all the information you can; copies of lab work or investigations carried out recently are extremely useful. Some patients show up at my office as a follow-up from the emergency room and cannot tell me what they were diagnosed with, what was done to them, or what medicines they were prescribed. In some cases I have to reschedule the appointment, especially when they come to me from a hospital I am not affiliated with. Please see aspects of the history taking covered in the beginning of the book.

The next step in the diagnostic process is the physical examination, and thereafter some investigations, starting with the noninvasive to the invasive. Some patients believe that blood work is invasive and that once blood is taken everything has been checked for. This is one of the greatest areas of patient error. There are at least a couple thousand tests that can be run on blood; we never run all the tests possible on a blood sample for many reasons. First, we would need a *lot* of blood to do this, and second, it would be just too expensive. The insurance company would not pay for tests that do not relate to the documented diagnosis. Finally, we would have a lot of red herrings and might end up barking up the wrong tree. For example, if you come to the office with a cough and fever, it wouldn't make sense to draw blood and test for a uric acid level to see if you have gout. These are totally unrelated, as if a car had an obvious tire problem and the mechanic dismantled the engine. What is the relationship?

In the case of an emergency, probably your initial contact with a physician will be in the emergency room, though in some cases the first contact is in the office. One of the main advantages of the emergency room over the office is the ability to carry out all the tests necessary in one setting and get the results immediately. One recent experience comes to mind. A long-standing patient of mine came to my office with signs and symptoms of a brain hemorrhage. I needed an urgent CT scan of her brain and spent at least thirty minutes trying to convince the insurance company why I needed one. Eventually I asked for the name of the lady in charge of the pre-certification process and told her if anything happened to my patient I would hold her responsible. This finally got her attention, and I got the authorization for the CT scan. My patient had the scan that afternoon and was in the operating room that evening as the neurosurgeon removed the bleeding in her brain. She is alive and well today. If she had gone to the emergency room instead of my office, she would have received the CT scan with less hassle and would be in the operating room faster.

At the end of the visit there are certain things you as the patient should know. Therefore I recommend that all patients or their representatives ask a few questions like the following:

- Do you have a confirmed diagnosis?
- Is it serious?
- Will I completely recover?
- What kind of complications should I look out for?
- What and how many medications will I be on and for how long?
- When or how soon should I see you or my primary care physician again?
- May I have copies of the blood work or X-rays you have done today for my records?
- Do you recommend I see a specialist?
- What health screening tests do I need?
- What immunizations do I need?
- What other recommendations do you have for me in order to prolong my life?

At the end of every visit with my patients in my office I usually ask them to summarize the visit and tell me exactly what I have recommended, including my instructions and advice. You will be surprised how little people can recall of the visit! On occasions when patients are accompanied by a family member, it is that person who usually interrupts to correct what the patient has said. This goes to confirm that when people are ill, their emotions are riding so high they do not listen well; and even when they do their ability to understand what they have been told is limited. Therefore I always repeat my instructions and ask the patient to recall the information again. I go through this cycle until the patient gets it right.

CHAPTER 2

Major Causes of Death

I will now talk about the leading causes of death in the United States, as well as possible ways of preventing them or at least diagnosing them early in order to decrease morbidity and possibly prolong life.

The Centers for Disease Control keeps data on the leading causes of death. The latest data at the time of printing this book is for the year 2007. The top ten leading causes of death for the year 2007 are as follows:

- Heart Disease
- Cancer
- Stroke
- Chronic lower respiratory diseases
- Accidents
- Alzheimer's dementia
- Diabetes
- Influenza and pneumonia
- Kidney disease
- Septicemia/infections

Heart Disease

Heart disease, as is implied, consists of all the things that can go wrong with the heart. We can begin with congenital heart disease, which occurs at birth, and then move on to structural or valvular heart disease, which can occur in adulthood as a result of rheumatic fever as a child, among other causes. Abnormal heart rhythms can also occur; these are called *arrhythmias*, and the reason they cause problems is because the heart is unable to deliver enough blood to tissues, especially vital organs.

The big one, however, is coronary artery disease. This results from blockages in the vessels supplying different parts of the heart leading to the death of the muscle being supplied by that artery. Coronary artery disease is not caused by one entity; there are various things that can act in synergy to cause it. These are together called *risk factors*, and the more of them you have the higher the chances of suffering from coronary artery disease.

There are non-modifiable risk factors for this disease, which means that there are some risk factors nothing can be done about, like family history, age, and gender. Unfortunately we cannot choose our parents, and we must do our best to know the diseases or ailments that affect or affected them. If you tell your doctor a first-degree relative died from a massive heart attack at an early age, that automatically puts you at a high risk. Your physician will begin to aggressively try to lower your own risk by paying close attention to your modifiable risk factors. Modifiable risk factors for coronary artery disease include high bad cholesterol and trig- lycerides, low good cholesterol, high blood pressure, smok- ing, obesity, sedentary lifestyle, and the big one—diabetes.

Most patients say they "feel fine" while their cholesterol, triglycerides, and blood pressures are through the roof. There are two types of cholesterol, the good and the bad. High-density lipoproteins, also known as HDL, are good cholesterol; the higher the better. A simple way to remem- ber this is that *h* is for *higher*. Should the HDL be *low*, that is in itself a problem and a risk factor. I have taken care of people who have suffered a heart attack, and the only thing we could find wrong was a very low level of good cholesterol. Your physician may decide to use medications to raise your HDL. Other things that can raise it include diet, exercise, omega-3 fatty acids, and certain vitamins and coenzymes, as well as red wine in *moderation*. The bad cholesterol is the low-density lipoprotein also known as LDL. The *l* stands for *lower*, the lower the better; this can be low- ered by diet, exercise, and medications. Triglycerides are also an important risk factor, and the way I explain them to my patients is that they are a cousin to cholesterol. A lot of patients tell me they have never heard of triglycerides and are surprised that they are a risk factor for coronary artery disease. Cholesterol and triglyceride levels are checked by taking a blood sample after an overnight fast with nothing to eat or drink for about eight hours.

What levels are good enough? Well, it depends on what else you have going on. Generally speaking, triglycerides should be less than 150 mg/dl, LDL less than 160mg/dl, and HDL over 45mg/dl in men and 55 in women. A common error is stopping your medications when the levels have come down—a big mistake! Once you have been diagnosed with an abnormal cholesterol level, the medications need to be continued for life. I usually use the analogy of pushing a car up a hill, but as soon as the car starts moving uphill you stop pushing. Then the car starts to roll down the hill in the opposite direction!

Should you have any side effects please stop the medications and let your doctor know so the medication can be replaced. This does not mean you should not take any type of cholesterol medicine anymore but that the type you were taking has to be stopped and an alternative you can tolerate will be started. Common and potentially serious side effects from the group of medications called statins are muscle cramps. When on these medications, periodic liver tests are needed, and the medications may have to be stopped if any abnormalities are detected. Liver function tests are also required as a baseline prior to starting the medications.

A common error is that patients feel dieting and exercise will *always* take care of their high cholesterol. This is not true; some cholesterol problems are genetic and therefore need more than diet and exercise to achieve control.

Another huge risk factor for coronary heart disease is blood pressure. High blood pressure is the same as hypertension. I have had patients tell me they have one and not the other. They are one and the same; you may call it which-ever is easier for you to pronounce or remember. I strongly suggest that every home have a blood pressure moni-tor. According to *Consumer Reports* magazine, the most reliable and accurate brand is the Wal-Mart store brand called ReliOn. The accuracy of your method of checking is another issue and can always be crosschecked by another machine or by your physician's office. In fact, I recommend that you take your blood pressure machine in to your doc-tor's office during your next appointment so its accuracy can be verified. Sometimes there is a very large margin of error. A patient of mine had a faulty blood pressure appa-ratus, and after several calls to me at varying times of the day and night I asked her to bring her machine into my office only to find out that it was about thirty to forty points higher than what it should be!

Hypertension is called the silent killer because a lot of people who have it do not know that they do. It may not manifest with any symptoms whatsoever, and a lot of times the first symptom is a stroke, a heart attack, or kidney failure. A lot of people need more than one medication to control their blood pressure. Many African-Americans may need up to three medications to adequately control their blood pressure. These days we have different combinations of blood pressure medications; some of them have three dif-ferent combinations in one, and it is now common to have two medications in one pill. A lot of the medications have side effects, but there are so many medications out there that your physician will be able to get one that works for you. Optimal blood pressure is less than 120/80; high blood pressure is anything above 140/90, and between the two is pre-hypertension.

People always ask me what else can be done to lower blood pressure apart from medications. My recommendations are exercise, weight loss, and diet change to a Mediterranean diet with grains and plenty of fruits and vegetables. Some of my patients ask about garlic and natural herbs. My advice is that I have seen too many people harm themselves trying to control their blood pressure by other means. Please always check your pressure to see if whatever you are taking is working, and if it is not then see your doctor immediately. A lot of these remedies are toxic to the body and can cause severe effects like kidney or liver failure.

If you have been diagnosed as having high blood pressure and do not have any health insurance, you can always ask your doctor to prescribe cheaper generic medications like the famous Wal-Mart list of four-dollar medications, which a lot of other pharmacy chains have matched in one form or the other. I must, however, sound a note of warning about a particular blood pressure medication that can cause rebound hypertension when it is stopped suddenly. The medication is clonidine, and if you are taking it, ensure you always have an adequate supply and do not miss any doses. Give your new blood pressure medicine time to work, and also let your body adjust to it before you abandon it; or tell your doctor you want to change medicine. Apart from being expensive, changing medications often exposes you to the risk of uncontrolled blood pressure during the transition period. A lot of people do not want to take medication for their blood pressure but are also not ready to do what is takes to limit or eliminate medications altogether.

So how can your physician help? You and your physician are partners; always tell him or her what you are experiencing. Do not leave your doctor's office with samples of medications that you know have given you a side effect in the past only to stop them. This results in an increase in your blood pressure and then a return visit to the doctor's office only for your blood pressure to be through the roof again bringing you right back to where you started from, resulting in a wasted visit for both of you. When a physician prescribes a medication you are having a side effect to, stop the medication and call your physician, who will prescribe an alternative. If you do not hear from your doctor within two days, call again and if need be swing by the office to get an alternative, preferably a sample so you are sure it works for you before you spend your hard-earned dollars on a prescription.

I cannot emphasize it enough: every home should have a blood pressure monitor. If you have any loved ones or elderly parents that you are responsible for, please buy them a blood pressure machine at your first opportunity. There are some guidelines for checking your blood pressure at home. It should be measured twice a day for a week every two to three months, and the blood pressure reading you get at home is generally lower than what is acceptable in the doctor's office which is considered a stressful place resulting in higher readings. If you feel dizzy after taking your blood pressure medicine, check your blood pressure before and after taking your medications and then call your doctor with that information; it might save you an office visit.

• Diabetes is another major cause of coronary heart disease and premature death. We will deal with it in detail in a section on its own because it is a major cause of death and disability and must be treated with a lot of respect.

Smoking is the next huge risk factor of coronary heart disease. As an ex-smoker I can tell you it is one of the most difficult habits to kick. I was blessed to be able to quit cold turkey, and I then avoided all my friends who are heavy smokers. There are several support groups and some prescription medications as well as over-the-counter ones like nicotine patches and gums, which can assist those who are willing to stop smoking. There are even some claims that acupuncture has helped some people. It is an extremely difficult habit to quit, and smokers need all the family support and encouragement they can get to assist them to kick the habit. It helps to set a quit date and inform your family and friends so they can help you to work towards it. Most of these people must be preferably nonsmokers. Some people can do it cold turkey while others need to gradually taper off.

The more risk factors you have, the higher the possibility of developing and dying from heart disease. There is a formula for calculating the ten-year risk of developing coronary artery disease. This is widely available on the Internet and is a tool your physician uses to help determine your risk.

Cancer

Cancer is the second leading cause of death in the United States. Women and men differ regarding the kind of cancer that afflicts them even though there are some cancers that are common to both sexes; early detection is the key to increased survival, and a lot of great screening tools are available for some of the cancers that cause the most death in this country and worldwide.

In most cases the diagnosis of cancer is made by taking a piece of the tissue involved or suspected and sending it to the lab. The lab will tell us if indeed it is a malignancy and what type it is. A professor of mine used to say that with cancer you cannot "treat without meat." Sometimes the way the lesions look either through an X-ray, a CT scan, or a camera may raise our suspicion that it looks like cancer, but we still need a piece of tissue in most cases to prove it. There is a relatively new imaging technique called a PET scan based on positron emission that can let physicians know with a high degree of certainty if a lesion is malignant or not.

To prevent **breast cancer**, a mammogram for all women age forty and over is recommended by the US preventive task force and should be carried out yearly or at least once every two years. Recently I was interviewing a new patient to my practice; she was sixty-six years old and had never heard of a mammogram. I promptly ordered one, and as things would turn out she had breast cancer. Thankfully she is doing well now, but please ask your physician about a mammogram starting at the age of forty in most cases and at thirty-five in some other situations, all depending on the family history. Your physician will let you know when to start.

I am aware of the recent controversy regarding screening mammograms, and just as other tasks forces have said, in my humble opinion it should be a decision between women and their physicians based on a lot of other factors. Even if it is said that screening saves only one life, would you not want that one person to be your sister, mother, daughter, cousin, or aunt? Having said that, some patients refuse to have one regardless. Some of these women are in the health care field, mostly nurses and a few physicians! Some say it is too painful, and others give the lame excuse that if they have cancer they do not want to know it! A lot of advances have been made in the field of radiology, and older women will tell you mammography today is in no way like it used to be. There have been advances in imaging techniques including digital imagery as well as Magnetic Resonance Imaging. Please encourage your loved ones to get a mammogram as soon as possible; an ounce of prevention is worth a pound of cure.

Cervical cancer has almost been eradicated in this country thanks to the aggressive screening of women. Yearly pap smears are recommended for women who are sexually active. Women have come to equate a pap to checking for sexually transmitted diseases. Some physicians screen for gonorrhea, chlamydia, yeast, and bacterial vaginal infections simultaneously, but the pap smear really checks for abnormal cervical cells. Depending on the patient's age as well as some other criteria, we may also screen for human papillomavirus, also known as HPV, which if infected with the right subtype increases the risk of cervical cancer. It is generally accepted that women should be screened for HPV by age eighteen. There is a vaccine recommended for young, sexually active females. I once had a woman at a health fair ask me if I would recommend it to my daughter, being that it is a relatively new vaccine. My answer, of course, is yes. I had the unfortunate experience of caring for a thirty-year-old female in the terminal phases of cervical cancer; it was indeed a very sad case. Screening for cervical cancer can be stopped in women over sixty-five years of age or women who have had adequate screening with negative results. Talk to your doctor about when to start or stop screening for you and your female family members.

Moving on to men, **prostate cancer** screening should be done from the age of forty, earlier in African-American men, who have a higher risk of developing prostate cancer. The annual prostatic specific antigen—PSA—is somewhat controversial but is being requested and carried out by most men and physicians. The interpretation of the test has changed over the years, and there is more emphasis being placed on the speed with which the PSA rises over months or years, also termed the velocity of the rise of the PSA. Not all elevated PSA is prostate cancer and not all prostate cancer results in an elevated PSA, but I have sent quite a few men to the urologist for a biopsy for a rapidly rising PSA and it turned out they had prostate cancer. Initially the men were skeptical because the PSA was normal, but they still went and are grateful they did.

The PSA is generally drawn before the rectal examination is done; if the rectal examination is done first, the PSA could be falsely elevated in some cases. The rectal exam is the male pap smear; it is unpleasant for both the patient and the doctor, but it is necessary to feel the consistency and size of the gland. Your physician will sometimes send you to the urologist for a biopsy when a prostate exam is abnormal; for instance, when we feel a lump or some irregularity in the gland. Men with a family history of prostate cancer should have increased surveillance.

Lung cancer is the leading cause of cancer death in both men and women. According to the American Cancer Society, it is projected to be the leading cause of cancer deaths in both men and women for 2008. Unfortunately, there is no effective screening test yet to diagnose lung cancer early. The major risk factor is smoking even though a lot of nonsmokers have unfortunately succumbed to the disease. Radon, an odorless, colorless, radioactive gas, has also been mentioned as a major risk factor. The main way to avoid lung cancer in a vast majority of the cases is to stop smoking and avoid secondhand smoke. I have witnessed a wife who never smoked develop lung cancer, while her husband who chain-smoked was cancer free!

Patients frequently tell me a relative of theirs chain-smoked and never got lung cancer. I have news for you— you are not that person! If ever you are told a "spot" was found on a chest X-ray, it has to be pursued to a logical conclusion. Your physician will order a CT scan or a PET scan and send you to a lung doctor—a pulmonologist. I have seen patients disappear after they are diagnosed with a spot on their lungs only to reappear with widespread cancer too late for treatment. We have lost two brilliant physicians in our community recently who never smoked in their lives. One of them was a brilliant pulmonologist who told me how ironic life was just before he died. In summary there is no screening test for lung cancer. Most of the cases are diagnosed incidentally while looking for something else. In most people by the time the cancer starts to result in symptoms like weight loss, coughing blood, and chest pains, the tumor has far advanced.

Colo-rectal cancer, as the name implies, affects the colon as well as the rectum. It is projected to be the third leading cause of cancer death in both males and females for the year 2008 according to the American Cancer Society. There are very good screening tests for this, including fecal occult blood testing and double contrast barium enema, as well as the gold standard, a colonoscopy. The first consists of testing stool samples for microscopic blood randomly. This is blood that cannot be seen by the naked eye, something like a slow-leaking tire; you know it is leaking but you cannot see the air escaping. The second test is a radiological test involving the administration of contrast into the rectum of a patient and taking some X-rays. If any of these tests is abnormal, the patient will be subjected to a colonoscopy. This involves taking some laxatives to clean out the colon and then having a scope passed through the anus to inspect the entire length of the colon. This test serves as a diagnostic as well as therapeutic procedure in some cases. The gastroenterologist or GI specialist who carries out the test is able to remove precancerous lesions that are sent to the lab for identification. Remember, "you cannot treat without meat."

Over the years I have had the displeasure of diagnosing colon cancer in patients who had previously refused a colonoscopy, but I have also had the fortune of catching early precancerous lesions in patients who were finally convinced to have a colonoscopy. The most common error is refusing a colonoscopy because of the "discomfort" of the laxative as well as the sedation required to carry out the test. As someone who has been subjected to the test, I can say, yes, it is uncomfortable, and I agree that the preparation for the test is far worse than the test itself, which is an invasive procedure with serious possible complications like bleeding, perforation, and infection. These rarely occur, however, and when they do they are in most cases rectifiable. Nowadays most perforations can be repaired by a pinhole incision. This is not to say that complications still do not occur, but we do not refuse to ride in a car just because someone we know died in an accident. The benefits of a colonoscopy outweigh the risks, and everyone should have one as soon as they reach the age of fifty or earlier depending on family history and other medical conditions.

Once the test is completely negative with no polyps whatsoever, then you have a ten-year wait for another test. In people with a family history of colon cancer in a first-degree relative less than sixty years of age, or an inherited disorder in which they develop a large amount of precancerous polyps, colonoscopies may be started in the teenage years or ten years younger than the age of onset of colon cancer in the youngest family member to be affected. The recommendations will depend on what the actual diagnosis of the family member was; therefore it is very important to know what the afflictions of all your first-degree relatives are if you can. You are always welcome to get a second opinion if you're not sure of what your GI doctor is telling you. Your primary care physician can always guide you in the right direction. The take-home message is to get a colonoscopy if you are over fifty! Medicine, unfortunately, is not one of those professions where you say, "If it ain't broke don't fix it!" If you don't fix it, it will most likely disable or kill you.

The fourth leading cause of cancer death in both men and women is **pancreatic cancer**. Unfortunately there is no good screening test for this form of deadly cancer. Like lung cancer, most of the time it is discovered as an incidental finding when we are looking for something else. In other cases it is discovered when it is way too late; in about half of these cases the cancer has spread by the time it is diagnosed. Depending on your source of information, there are many risk factors involved in the development of pancreatic cancer. Yes, smoking is one of them; others are diabetes, obesity, heavy alcohol use, age, and chronic pancreatitis. This cancer is extremely difficult to treat, and some describe it as one of the most painful cancers on earth.

A very common error that occurs in patients and their families after being told there is no more medical science can offer is to hang on to the hopes of alternative medicine. I have seen families spend their life savings on alternative medical care treatments with outrageous claims to cure, but in fact these are scams that rip people off of all their life savings. One family I knew borrowed a huge amount of money to take the wife to Georgia from Michigan for alternative medical care. She ended up deteriorating faster than was predicted and eventually died. The husband had to borrow money to transport his family back home after spending his family's life savings. Find out what medications are going to be used and research them yourself before allowing anybody to inject them into you or your loved one. I know we want to hang on to hope by all means, and this is what the individuals that push this type of treatment rely on. Always have a family member or friend who is not emotionally involved to be your voice of reason in situations like this.

Stroke

The third leading cause of death in the USA is stroke; there are about seven hundred thousand cases of stroke on a yearly basis according to the American Stroke Association. About two hundred thousand of these cases occur among people with recurrent stroke. A number of people with transient ischemic attacks or "mini strokes" have an increased risk of having another stroke. Most strokes are due to blood clots; a few others are due to a bleed in the substance of the brain. Most recommendations for the prevention of a stroke therefore focus on the type of stroke caused by a blood clot.

You will notice that the risk factors for heart disease are almost identical to those for stroke. Risk factors for stroke include the following.

Hypertension: There are about fifty million Americans with high blood pressure, a lot of whom do not know they have it, and even those who do know frequently have blood pressures that are not well controlled. With good blood pressure control you can lower your risk of a stroke by 30 to 40 percent, but I have found patients to be very reluctant to take blood pressure pills. This is because they usually have no symptoms, and hypertension is called the silent killer. In many cases the very first sign of hypertension is a stroke. Some patients tell me they always have a high blood pressure. This is something to be concerned about, and should be acted on by every adult individual. Again, my recommendation is that every family should have a blood pressure machine at home, even if you have already been diagnosed with hypertension. Whenever your blood pressure or that of a significant other or loved one is persistently over 140/90, please seek medical attention immediately.

Please talk to your healthcare provider to determine what your target blood pressure is. Diabetics need to have a lower blood pressure target than the general population. It is generally agreed that a diabetic should have a blood pressure of no more than 130/80; this number could be lower depending on other problems you might have. Unfortunately most people will need more than one blood pressure medication to get their pressures under control, and as I mentioned before, a lot of people stop their medications because they develop adverse reactions to them. For instance, men often complain that the medications cause erectile dysfunction. Remember, there are hundreds of blood pressure medications available; surely there will be one that you can tolerate. No one should stop their blood pressure medication without getting a replacement from their physician. Having no insurance is no excuse; your physician can control your pressure with a combination of medications from the four-dollar list a lot of pharmacies have now; we can also help you out with samples, and a lot of the pharmaceutical companies have a medication assistance program to help people who cannot afford medications. Try to take the medications at the same time every day and ensure you have refills, especially when going out of town.

Blood pressure medicines, like diabetes treatment and treatment for cholesterol, are for life in most cases. Your physician can decide to take you off medication if he or she feels your blood pressure is well controlled without it. This can happen in people who lose weight and stop drinking or smoking. Generally speaking, a twenty-pound weight loss can lead to an eight-point drop in the top number of the blood pressure reading. Other ways to help lower blood pressure include a diet rich in fruits, vegetables, and grains, regular exercise, and reduction of dairy products.

Whatever you do, monitor your blood pressure regularly so you know if what you are doing or what you are taking is not working. Mrs. Y had been a patient of mine for about three years. She had very difficult-to-control blood pressure and had refused to see a cardiologist to assist in her blood pressure management. She wanted to avoid seeing "too many doctors." I tried a lot of different classes of blood pressure medications, but each time she came back in the office her blood pressure was still out of control. I checked her out for other causes of high blood pressure, and all the tests were negative, but she is extremely obese, which did not help the situation. She is very highly educated and so she understood the consequences of uncontrolled blood pressure, and she always came to the office with near perfect readings of her blood pressure at home; thus she self-diagnosed herself as having "white coat" hypertension.

I got a call from the emergency room one day telling me Mrs. Y had suffered a stroke! I admitted her and went through the complete stroke evaluation, which led to the conclusion that her stroke was secondary to uncontrolled blood pressure. Remarkably, however, her blood pressure while in hospital was very well controlled with only three of her four medications. She was also extremely lucky that her stoke was very mild and left her with minimal deficits. We discharged her, and she saw me in the office on follow-up after about two weeks, accompanied by her daughter. As soon as she saw me she burst into tears, I wondered what was amiss, and her daughter encouraged her to tell me "the truth." Then Mrs. Y told me she had been deceiving me regarding her blood pressure readings as well as her medications. She never took *any* of the medications I prescribed for her. She flushed her daily dosages down the toilet because she knew I would count the pills left in her bottle at every visit, and she also made up her blood pressure readings! She now promised to follow my advice to the letter because the stroke really scared her and she did not want to have another one. I could not believe it, but I accepted her apology and am happy to tell you her blood pressure is under excellent control now and she is scheduled to have lap band soon for her morbid obesity after going through a rigorous medical clearance. Sometimes patients need a life-altering event to jolt them into reality. I only hope the event does not result in residual lifelong problems.

Diabetes: Another risk factor for stroke, diabetes affects about 8 percent of the adult population. The control of blood pressure in diabetics has been shown to reduce the risk of stroke significantly. The control of diabetes has also been shown to reduce the large and small vessel complications of diabetes. This disease is so significant that I have dedicated a separate section to talking about the most common mistakes patients make when it comes to the treatment and control of this dreaded ailment. Diet, exercise, oral medications, and insulin-like shots, as well as insulin are the mainstay of diabetes treatment.

High cholesterol and triglycerides: Remember, triglycerides are a cousin to cholesterol and therefore a risk factor in heart disease as well. The ten-year risk of developing a stroke is calculated based on triglycerides and the level of your cholesterol. The recommendations in a high-risk person, like someone who has already suffered a stroke or has heart disease, is to lower bad cholesterol to under 100, preferably 70. The higher the good cholesterol, the better; over 40 is ideal. Triglycerides should be less than 150, and lipids are always estimated after an overnight fast.

Cigarette smoking: This is a tough one, and as a former smoker I can identify with the difficulty involved with kicking the habit. The risks involved in smoking subside after quitting the habit for five years. The avoidance of environmental tobacco is also recommended.

Alcohol consumption: Drinking is also a risk factor, especially heavy drinking, even though moderate alcohol consumption is regarded by most people as a negative risk for stroke.

Age: The older you are the more likely you are to suffer a stroke.

Obesity: People with a body mass index over 30 are especially at risk for a stroke. This also goes hand in hand with a lot of other risk factors like hypertension, diabetes, cholesterol, and abdominal obesity. A waist circumference of over forty inches in males and thirty-five inches in females is an independent risk for stroke.

Physical Inactivity: At least thirty minutes of physical activity on most days, or about 150 minutes of physical activity per week, is recommended to reduce the risk of stroke.

Chronic Lower Respiratory Disease

This is the fourth leading cause of death in the US; this entity is also sometimes referred to as chronic obstructive pulmonary disease, also known as COPD. This is a progressive disease and includes chronic bronchitis and emphysema or any combination. About twelve million Americans have the disease, but it is thought to be under diagnosed. Annual costs are estimated at approximately thirty-seven billion dollars as direct and indirect costs. The way I describe it to my patients is the difference between blowing air into a balloon and into a paper bag. The balloon has immediate recoil while the paper bag holds on to the air in a phenomenon called "air trapping." The diagnosis is confirmed by spirometer in your doctor's office; this is a very simple, non-invasive test and can also be used to monitor the progress of the disease. It measures lung volume and the amount of air that can be expelled forcefully in one second, among other measurements. In some cases your primary care physician will refer you to a pulmonologist.

Certain factors contribute to COPD, like smoking, a family history of the disease, and the absence of a protein that helps to keep the air sacs in the lung open. Some airways are hyper responsive; exposure to dusts and chemical pollution and recurrent air pollution are also contributing factors. Your physician will assess you for home oxygen, and if you qualify it will be ordered for you. Home oxygen helps to prolong life and should be worn for as many hours as is recommended.

A patient of mine was greatly embarrassed about wearing her oxygen especially when she was shopping. She felt all eyes were on her, and this was a great source of distress to her. She finally found comfort in the very small, portable tanks that could supply enough oxygen for short periods of time. Please talk to your physician if this social stigma is preventing you or your loved one from complying with medical advice. There are also combinations of inhalers that are used for the treatment of this disease.

Stopping the use of tobacco is the single most important thing to do to stop the progression of COPD. If you continue to smoke your lungs will continue to deteriorate. I have had a couple of patients continue to smoke while on oxygen; one burned his fingers, the other burned most of his house, and the third unfortunately killed himself. Please do not smoke while on oxygen; the two are incompatible!

Oral and inhaled steroids are used very frequently in the treatment of these diseases, and everyone with COPD should have a flu shot yearly and a pneumonia shot once in five years. This tends to reduce the incidence of serious illnesses, respiratory failure, and death. Cigarette smoking accounts for over 90 percent of COPD cases. If you are on steroids often your physician may prescribe calcium and vitamin D supplements to prevent osteoporosis in the future.

Accidents

The fifth cause of death in the US, accounting for over one hundred thousand deaths in the year 2007, can be attributed to car accidents. It therefore follows that to reduce the chances of dying in a motor vehicle accident you should always wear a seat belt, avoid over speeding, and avoid driving or being driven by anyone who is intoxicated. Other accidents include firearms, poisoning, suffocation, and falls, especially in the elderly. The Institute of Medicine recently convened a panel to identify behavioral and cognitive strategies to prevent motor vehicle accidents in teenagers, usually caused by drinking, the lack of use of seat belts, not getting adequate sleep, and not knowing the rules of the road.

Diabetes

According to the World Health Organization more than 220 million people worldwide have diabetes. In the USA the CDC estimates that a total number of 23.4 million people have diabetes out of which 17.9 million are diagnosed and 5.7 million are undiagnosed. In 2005, an estimated 1.1 million people died from diabetes. Almost 80 percent of diabetes deaths worldwide occur in low- and middle-income countries, and almost half of diabetes deaths occur in people under the age of seventy years; 55 percent of diabetes deaths are in women. WHO projects that diabetes death will double between 2005 and 2030.

Normal blood sugar in the United States is less than 100 mg per deciliter (mg/dl); when your fasting blood sugar is over or equal to 126 mg/dl you are diabetic. If two hours after eating your blood sugar is over 200 and you have symptoms of diabetes, then you are diabetic. If, however, your fasting blood sugar is between 100 and 125mg/dl, you have what we call "prediabetes," and if aggressive measures are not implemented you will become diabetic. Healthy diet, regular physical activity, maintaining a normal body weight, and avoiding tobacco use can prevent or delay the onset of diabetes.

There are two types of diabetes, type 1 and type 2. Type 1 mostly requires insulin, while type 2 generally does not. Type 2 is usually a slower onset type of the disease and used to be seen in individuals over forty, but now it is becoming prevalent in younger adults and teenagers because of childhood obesity. Ninety to ninety-five percent of diabetes worldwide is type 2. There are other types of diabetes, such as during pregnancy, as well as a type that is secondary to other factors, for instance, the use of steroids. This, of course, is a gross oversimplification of this complex illness that has scientists all over the world struggling to find a cure.

If you have been diagnosed with diabetes by your doctor, what next? There are certain questions you need to ask.

For instance, you need to know if you are a type 1 or a type 2 diabetic. Even though there is an overlap in some cases and a lot of type 2 diabetics need to be on insulin, your doctor will be able to tell you. Some individuals can control the diabetes with diet and exercise alone. These people have a critical weight over which they will be symptomatic. Some need medications, and others need injections of insulin or insulin-like shots.

Diabetes is a very challenging disease, and if you do not treat it with the respect it deserves you will be sentenced to hospital with a lot of complications and may eventually lose your vital organs, limbs, or your life to it. I have seen blood sugars as high as 1800 in a newly diagnosed diabetic who came to the hospital in coma. If you do not check your blood sugar, how do you know it is high? A lot of patients tell me they can "feel it," and I tell them in turn they should always confirm their feelings by checking the blood sugar.

My father had a patient who was a butcher who came to our house every morning initially and then twice a day thereafter. He had told my father he noticed that anytime he passed urine ants swarmed his urine; I do not mean to gross you out, but he tasted his urine and found it was sweet, and that is how he ended up with my father for treatment. He eventually became blind from what we now know is diabetic retinopathy and eventually died most likely from kidney failure.

One of the first things you *must* do after being diagnosed is to go for diabetic teaching by a certified diabetes educator. Most hospitals have them, or you can search online for classes through the American Diabetic Association. You want to learn how to check your blood sugar and what it means. You have to understand what foods to eat and what to stay away from. You need to be able to estimate the amount of carbohydrates in each meal you consume. You must understand the signs and symptoms of low blood sugar and what to do when you have it. You must know how to check your blood sugar regularly and record it in a log to take to your doctor. Initially at diagnoses you need to check your blood sugar fasting two hours after each meal and before you go to bed.

Generally speaking your blood sugar should be between 80 and 120 when you have not had anything to eat in the morning, less than 180 two hours after a meal, and between 100 and 140 at bedtime. Of course, if you are newly diagnosed, you will need frequent visits as well as calls to your physician until you achieve these goals. The only people who are exempted from these numbers are individuals with "brittle" diabetes; their blood sugars vary widely within a short period of time, and they have an increased risk of low blood sugar, which is very dangerous and can lead to permanent brain damage. Physicians often prefer to avoid low blood sugars, which are generally more dangerous than the high ones. In order to avoid this situation in people with labile diabetes, we sometimes allow the blood sugars to be on the higher side in these individuals to avoid episodes of low blood sugar.

The next thing is to know your glycosylated hemoglobin, popularly referred to as A1C. This number tells you how well you have been doing in controlling your blood sugar over the past three months. The target is 6.5; again, your doctor may allow yours to be a bit higher if you are at a higher risk of hypoglycemia. The next thing that you should do at diagnosis is to have a dilated eye examination by your ophthalmologist, who will look at the back of your eye to ensure there is no bleeding; if there is he or she knows how to fix it. This eye exam should be done yearly.

The next thing is to monitor your blood pressure. A diabetic's blood pressure needs to be under stricter control—130/80 is the target for diabetics because it lowers the risk of heart problems and kidney problems. Cholesterol levels need to be monitored regularly; LDL should be less than 100, triglycerides should be less than 150, and HDL should be over 45 in men and 55 in women.

Diabetics should also have their feet examined regularly and visit a podiatrist once a year. I remember examining the foot of a diabetic earlier in my career only to find a nail in the sole of his foot that he did not know was there! Diabetics lose sensation in their feet and therefore do not feel pain like non-diabetics. It is therefore important that diabetics inspect their feet every morning for early signs of infection. It is amazing how rapidly infections can spread in a diabetic. I have seen a lot of diabetics lose their digits and limbs because they waited too late to seek help. If you are diabetic, the slightest sign of an infection should prompt you to seek medical advice immediately. Even after being started on an antibiotic, keep an eye on the infection to ensure it is clearing. If in three days it is not better, go back to your doctor; do not sit at home.

Diabetics also need to have their urine examined once a year for protein, as diabetes is the most common cause of kidney failure. One of the earliest signs of kidney failure is protein in the urine. If your doctor notices this he or she will put you on a family of blood pressure medications called angiotensin-converting enzymes, ACE for short. I usually have a lot of patients giving me a very hard time about the use of this medicine. They say it is a blood pressure pill, and they do not have high blood pressure; but remember my explanation in the previous discussion of blood pressure. This medicine may cause some adverse reactions like a cough; when this happens we change to a cousin of this medication that will have the same beneficial effects; these are called angiotensin-receptor blockers, or ARBS. As far as I know only one ARB is generic now, but almost all ACE inhibitors are generic and are therefore cheaper.

Diabetics should take an aspirin a day and complete all their adult immunizations, especially the annual flu shot as well as pneumococcal vaccine shots. The tetanus shot is also recommended, and this is usually combined with the diphtheria and pertussis vaccine, a disease that has recently seen an increase in adults. After age sixty-five, diabetics are encouraged to get the shingles vaccine.

49

There are a lot of complications in diabetes that can be life threatening. As I always tell my patients, death as an end point is inevitable for us all. What really matters is how we die and how much suffering and morbidity we face before the end finally comes. Good control of diabetes can delay the onset of complications and in some cases prevent them altogether. Things still happen, but when complications do occur, you want to be certain that you did your best. In summary being a diabetic means you need to pay attention to detail. This is a good foundation to build on with the guidance and assistance of your doctor. Learn more about your disease and ask questions so you are educated about it.

CHAPTER 3

Medications

We now have a fairly good idea of what the common causes of death in this country are. We also have an idea of how to avoid them or at best manage them. We will now spend some time discussing the medications used to manage these conditions, and others.

At some point in our lives we will have to take medications. This may be for a short period of time, an extended period, intermittently, or continuously for the rest of our lives. Taking medications can be a challenge. I came to this conclusion over twenty-five years ago while I was in medical school. At that time I was put on antibiotics to be taken four times a day for two weeks. I almost went crazy! At that time we did not have things like cell phones we could program to sound an alert when it was time to take the medication. I could not wait for the two weeks to be over. Now I am grateful I take only one medication daily, and even that is a challenge to me. I therefore have a lot of sympathy for my patients, some of whom could be on up to thirty pills a day!

The first thing I do when I come across a new patient with a lot of medicines is to go through the medication bag with the patient and discontinue all nonessential medicines. One thing that must be avoided in dealing with elderly patients especially is poly-pharmacy. Elderly patients make up about 12 percent of the US population and account for about 35 percent of all prescription medications! During my residency I had the opportunity to be trained by one of the nation's leading geriatricians—a specialist in the care of the elderly—and he told me that one of his secrets of success as a geriatrician was discontinuing a lot of medications among the elderly and not adding more. I have continued to practice this with great rewards for my elderly patients. I adhere to the motto of "one disease, one drug, one time a day," where possible, of course.

The Beers criteria were developed by a US consensus panel of experts; according to them there are many medications that should generally be avoided or used with extreme caution in persons over sixty-five years of age because they are either ineffective or may create an unnecessarily high risk for adverse events. An updated Beers list by D.M. Fick, J.W. Cooper, W.E. Wade, et al, is given below. All medications are listed as their pharmaceutical names.

This list should not be considered in isolation, and each patient situation is unique, so always consult with your physician to determine the risk, benefits and possible alternatives for any of these medications.

Pain Medications

Indomethacin

Ketorolac

Meperidine

Naproxen

Oxaprozin

Pentazocine

Piroxicam

Propoxyphene (has since been taken off the US market)

Stimulants

Amphetamine mixtures

Dextroamphetamine

Methamphetamine

Appetite Suppressants

Benzphetamine

Diethylypropion

Phendimetrazine

Phentermine

Antidepressants

Amitriptyline

Doxepin

Fluoxetine

Antihistamines

Chlorpheniramine

Cyproheptadine

Dexchorpheniramine

Diphenhydramine

Hydroxyzine
Promethazine

Antipsychotics
Thioridazine
Mesoridazine

Barbiturates
Amobarbital
Butabarbital
Mephobarbital
Pentobarbital
Secobarbital

Sedatives
Chlordiazepoxide
Diazepam
Quazepam
Halazepam
Chlorazepate
Flurazepam
Alprazolam (more than 2 mg)
Lorazepam (more than 3 mg)
Oxazepam (more than 60 mg)
Temazepam (more than 15 mg)
Triazolam (more than 0.25 mg)

Heart Medicine
Amiodarone
Disopyramide
Methyldopa
Nifedipine (short acting)

Gastrointestinal Medications

Belladonna alkaloids

Clidinium-chlordiazepoxide

Dicyclomine

Hyoscyamine

Propantheline

Laxatives

Bisacodyl

Cascara sagrada

Castor oil

Mineral oil

Muscle relaxants

Carisoprodol

Chlorzoxazone

Cyclobenzaprine

Metaxalone

Orphenadrine

Urinary Antispasmodic

Oxybutinin

Others

Chlorpropamide

Desiccated thyroid

Meprobamate

Methyl testosterone

Nitrofurantoin

Ticlopidine

Trimethobenzamide

As we age, our bodies change not only outwardly but also on the inside. The way our bodies handle medications changes, and because of these changes we tend to be more susceptible to side effects or adverse effects of some medications. Some of the changes that occur in the aging body include decreased salivary flow accompanied by several other changes in the GI tract that lead to decreased absorption. There is also a change in the fat, muscle, and water content of the body. The resultant effect of this is that water- and fat-soluble drugs have an increase in their half-life. Also, some medications have an increase in the availability of the active byproduct of the medicine. Because of a decline in blood flow to the liver and kidneys, the medications are not eliminated as fast as they should, resulting in a longer duration of action. Since the elderly are the fastest-growing segment of the population as well as the largest users of prescription medications, there is an increase in the incidence of adverse reaction to medications. This is a cause of increased morbidity as well as mortality in the United States. According to some sources, the unwanted side effects of drugs are seven times more common in older patients than in the younger adults.

Therefore, anyone who has elderly relatives should pay a close attention to the medications that they are taking. Watch your loved one closely when a new medicine is prescribed. Be quick to stop the medication first and then call the physician to let him or her know about the side effects you suspect are manifesting in your loved one. In some cases when the use or discontinuation of the medication is not critical to the health of your loved one, your physician may suggest you stop the medicine for about one week and see if the symptoms go away; if they do you can restart the medicine to see if the adverse reactions return. This is my so-called stop-start-stop challenge.

There are certain strategies that have been documented to help reduce polypharmacy as well as adverse drug reactions. The patient's medications should be taken to every doctor's visit, and the only replacement for this should be a comprehensive list of medications including the strength, dosage, frequency, and the number of refills left. This list should include over-the-counter medications as well as herbs and supplements. Medications should be classified into lifelong medicines and those to be used to relieve a symptom. Medications that are used to relieve a symptom should be stopped at the first opportunity. Make sure you or your physicians are not making the mistake of treating the adverse reaction of one drug with another medication. In circumstances where possible, most physicians would prescribe medications once a day in the elderly to treat each illness or complaint. There are various medications identified by several specialists that should be prescribed with caution in the elderly. Refer to the previous section for a list, which is by no means exhaustive.

I must, however, be quick to caution that the printout of side effects of medications that is given to all of us when we pick up our medicines from the pharmacy should probably be read only after taking the medicine. Some people develop every single side effect listed because they read it could occur. Also, remember that your physician can be prescribing you a certain medication for an "off label" use. This is a use that has not been approved by the FDA, but due to experience your physician knows it may work for your particular circumstance.

Another issue is the dosage of the medicine. I have had several patients ask me what the dosage of the medication I prescribe for them is. When I inquire why, they reply they would like a very small dose. I want everyone to realize that the potency of the medication is what is important, not the dosage. For example, there are some diabetic medications that may be prescribed at a dosage of 1000 mg twice a day while others are prescribed in multiples of 4 or 5 milligrams, and they may be equivalent in potency. This applies to blood pressure medications as well; some like clonidine are prescribed in multiples of 1/10 of a milligram while some others like labetalol are prescribed in multiples of 200 mg with a maximum of 2400 mg a day. These two medications may be equivalent in their ability to lower blood pressure in several individuals; it would be a grave error to assume that the higher the dosage, the more potent a medication is.

The way I explain this to patients is that the amount of alcohol in a glass of beer is far less than in a glass of whiskey, even though they are the same quantity; but you would be making a grave mistake if you felt that, drinking a glass of beer without any problem, you could down the same quantity of whiskey! Therefore, the dosage of the medication is not as important as the potency, and questions about dosage are only relevant when comparing apples to apples, which in most cases is only when referring to the same medication.

A lot of my patients who are seeing me for the first time for control of their blood pressure inform me they have not been able to tolerate several blood pressure medications; when I ask which ones there is a long, deafening pause. The danger in this is that I may prescribe the same medication the patient tried in the past and did not like or that gave him or her unbearable side effects. The best thing to do is to keep a list of medications tried in the past that have either not helped or have caused you some adverse reactions. Yes, your physician can get the information from your medical records at your previous physician, but that will result in a delay of your care. You have to fill out a form authorizing the release of the medical information, which will be sent to the office of your previous health care provider, and these records can take at least a week to get to the new physician, who then has to go through it. I have been on the receiving end of a patient's file that was ten inches thick! So tell me, where do I start? You will be doing yourself a great service by keeping a list of all these medications.

Also, be aware of medications that have to be monitored by blood work regularly to ensure they do not exceed a certain threshold. Be aware of medications that require monitoring of certain organs for toxicity. One of the most common medications that needs to be monitored by regular blood work is the blood thinner Coumadin, also known as warfarin. Depending on why you are taking this medication, the blood level has to be within a certain range; also, there are several foods and other medications that can interact with it. For example, leafy green vegetables can lower the efficacy of warfarin, while antibiotics like levaquin can potentiate the effects. Other very common medications that have to be monitored by their blood levels include digoxin as well as antiseizure medications and some antirejection medicines in patients who have received organ transplants. There are numerous other medications that need to be monitored either directly or indirectly. This is another reason to keep your appointment regularly with your physician.

A group of medications whose toxicity needs to be monitored at least every three to six months is the group called statins, which help to lower cholesterol. Some patients use this as an excuse not to take statins, saying they do not want their liver damaged. I want to emphasize that medicine as a whole involves questions about risk and benefit in a lot of situations. Lowering cholesterol has a lot of benefits, including reducing the risk of stroke and heart disease; you cannot ignore this benefit because it *may* cause liver damage or severe muscle injury that may lead to kidney failure. Vehicle accidents kill hundreds of thousands of people yearly worldwide, but vehicles are an essential part of life in the twenty-first century. The fact that cars *may* crash, leading to severe injuries, does not mean we should avoid them altogether. What we try to do is reduce our risk of being involved in a crash by doing smart things like not drinking and driving, using seat belts, not speeding, etc. For the same reason some people avoid planes, because they may crash, but air transportation is one of the safest means available. During a recent major US holiday a news agency reported twenty-five thousand planes over the US air space that day, and I did not hear of any plane crash on that day.

Monitoring your liver function during the administration of statins will enable your physician to be proactive in assessing the damage to your liver. If you stay away from your physician for several months while taking medications that may cause adverse effects, it may be too late to reverse these effects when they are picked up. You may have reached the point of no return. This sets off a chain reaction because then your family members hear about this and swear they will not take any cholesterol pills because of what they did to you. They have drawn a conclusion without knowing what the exact facts are.

Some medications your physician will prescribe to you need to be monitored directly by checking the blood levels of the medication or indirectly by checking the effect of the medication on other systems. One of the most common Medications I have mentioned is warfarin. This medication can be lifesaving in certain situations and circumstances, but it has to be monitored regularly. If you are taking warfarin and you have not had the blood level checked in over four weeks, stop reading this book now and see your physician *tomorrow* to have the level checked. I have had some patients defect to my practice from other primary care physicians complaining to me that their previous physician did not "know what he is doing" only because he was changing the dose of the Coumadin frequently in accordance to the level of the patient's international normalized ratio, or INR. The level at which the INR should be—usually referred to as the "target range"—depends on what is being treated. For example, when treating a blood clot in the lungs or legs, the target is usually between 2 and 3. In other patients, like those with a mechanical heart valve, the recommended range could be as high as between 3 and 4. Warfarin is broken down differently by different people, some very quickly and others very slowly. Unless some form of genetic testing is done, it is difficult to know what group an individual belongs to; therefore the proof of the pudding is in its eating. We have to start low and go slowly to see how each individual responds to the medication initially. As I have said, warfarin also interacts with a *ton* of medications as well as various food items, the most commonly known being leafy green vegetables. I admitted a nurse once for a blood clot in her legs and got her INR up to about 1.6, and I was pretty certain that she would go home the next day because my target was between 2 and 3. Lo and behold the next day the INR dropped to 1.4! I initially thought it was a laboratory error and asked for it to be repeated, but it came back the same. She had, of course, been given the Coumadin teaching package, and since she was a nurse I was certain she has more knowledge than any other member of the public. Anyway, after checking her medications and ensuring there was no adverse interaction, I questioned her about what she had been eating. She told me I would be proud of her and that she had decided to change her lifestyle while in the hospital; from the previous lunchtime she had been eating nothing but leafy salads. Her husband even went to a fast food restaurant the night before and bought her more salad! I was shocked that she did not realize she was reversing the effects of the warfarin by consuming all that salad. I asked if she had read the package, and she told me she was waiting to get home before reading it! Somehow she was also missed by the dietary department as well as the pharmacist, both of whom would automatically see a patient newly started on warfarin. Needless to say, her healthy eating habits kept her in hospital for three more days! Whenever you are taking warfarin or any other medication that can cause bleeding, you have to let *all* your physicians and dentists know, and of course, the effect must be monitored regularly on a schedule to be determined by your physician.

Another broad group of medications that have to be monitored regularly are medications used to prevent seizures. It's needless to say how important these medications are. If blood levels are too low, the individual may have a seizure; if the levels are too high they may induce very unpleasant side effects. Some medications used after organ transplants are also monitored for the same reason. Some medications have a very narrow therapeutic window, meaning that the dosage that makes you feel better is very close to the dose that can cause side effects. One of these medications is digoxin, a heart medicine; it also has to be monitored very closely.

Sometimes with very close supervision your doctor may notice that you are developing adverse reactions to medications. For example, some patients of mine developed kidney or liver dysfunction secondary to a medication, and I then instructed them to stop the medication. Most of the time I prefer to have the patient come into the office with all the medications currently being taken so I can use a marker to put a big mark on the medication that should be stopped. Do not throw away the medication that your doctor discontinues because he or she may ask you to start taking it again sometime in the future, so always take all your medications with you to your doctor at every visit. Whenever this is not possible, write down the medication, dosage, and frequency; the prescribing physician; and the number of refills left on your home medication list. This is to assist your physician and also ensure you get the most out of your visit.

In most cases after you stop a medication your physician will replace it with another one. This is very unlike the situation where you are on one blood pressure pill that is not doing the work, and your physician decides to add another medication to the one you are already taking. Most patients end up stopping the pill they are taking, mistaking the directions for a "replacement" not an "addition." I will again use the analogy of a broken-down vehicle that is being pushed by a good Samaritan. Unfortunately he is not strong enough to move the car, and so a few more good Samaritans lend a helping hand. Now when the car starts to move, the person who feels he is contributing the least to the pushing of the car stops because his effort is negligible. This also occurs in the case of the control of chronic diseases like hypertension and diabetes. We continue to add medications until we achieve our desired goal. Now, after achieving control we may discontinue one medication that we feel is the weak link in the effort to achieve control. Some people stop taking their medications altogether, or in the case of insulin go back to a previous dose even after getting to goal. I always hear patients asking me if they can stop all their medications because their blood pressure, blood sugar, or cholesterol is now within normal. Let us for a moment turn our attention back to the vehicle that is being pushed by several good Samaritans, who now realize their collective effort is being rewarded because the car is moving. They all realize this and stop pushing the car at the same time. What happens to the car? It stops moving, of course, and if they were going uphill the car rapidly returns to its origin or some point. I have seen this happen numerous times: we struggle to achieve goal, and once it is achieved we want to abandon the medications that got us there in the first place.

I remember a very pleasant older gentleman who happened to be a pastor at a local church who was referred to me by his niece, a nurse I worked with at one of the hospitals where I attended. His diabetes was way out of control, and on his first visit I painstakingly went through a new insulin regimen with him where he would adjust his own insulin every three days until he achieved the targets I set for him. I asked him and his wife to repeat what I had told them and also tested them with various scenarios; by the time they left I was confident his blood sugar would be controlled on his follow-up visit. I looked forward to seeing them again after two weeks, and before I eagerly walked into the exam room I peeped into his chart to see what his blood sugar in the office that afternoon was. To my utter shock, amazement, and disappointment his blood sugar was in the 300 range! Normal blood sugar is between 80 and 120. I walked into the exam room, and the pastor and his wife had wide grins on their faces. I enquired what had happened; my pastor patient and his wife told me the formula had worked perfectly and his blood sugar before he ate anything was in the low hundreds. So what happened today? He said he went back to the previous insulin dose. When I asked why he said I had not instructed him to stay at that dosage! I said, "Pastor, why did you leave the Promised Land after you got there?" He understood me immediately and has been very well controlled since then. Please, when asked by your physician to increase the dose of your medicine, do not go back to the previous dose without talking to him or her first.

Drug Confusion

Picking up your prescription at the pharmacy is just like picking up your food order at the carry out. You always have to check that what you ordered is what you pick up *before* you leave the pharmacy. When you get to the pharmacy, please ensure the medication that is prescribed is the one that is dispensed to you. I had a mentally challenged diabetic patient for whom I prescribed a diabetic medicine in the name of Glucotrol at ten milligrams twice a day. The pharmacist somehow dispensed Coumadin, a blood thinner, at the same dosage! Ten milligrams of Coumadin twice a day is a whopping dose, which should have prompted a call from the pharmacist to the physician. Anyway, when I saw my patient a week later I caught the error because as a rule my patients bring in *all* the medications they take to the office at every visit. Luckily the patient was noncompliant and was taking only one pill a day. We promptly checked how thin her blood was in the office and asked her to get some vitamin K to reverse the effect of the blood thinner. She went back to the same pharmacy and the prescription was wrongly filled again! I had no choice but to file a complaint against this particular pharmacy. Most pharmacists are on top of things and have helped on numerous occasions to call my attention to potential adverse reactions or drug interactions, and this was a very isolated incident.

Below is a list of lookalike/sound-alike medications taken from the January 25, 2010, issue of *Endocrine Today* journal. This list is not complete, and a complete list can be obtained from the Institute for Safe Medication Practices or the US Pharmacopeia at www.usp.org.

ACCOLATE—ACCUPRIL
ACCUTANE—ACCOLATE
ACETYLCYSTEINE—ACETAZOLAMIDE

ADDERALL—INDERAL

ADVAIR—ADVICOR

AMOXICILLIN—ATARAX

AZITHROMYCIN—AZTREONAM

AZMACORT—NASACORT

CEFAZOLIN—CEFPROZIL

CEFEPIME—CEFOTAN

CEFOTAXIME—CEFTAZIDIME

CIPROFLOXACIN—CEPHALEXIN

CLONIDINE—KLONOPIN

DIFLUCAN—DIPRIVAN

FAMOTIDINE—FLUOXETINE

FLONASE—FLOMAX

HYDROMORPHONE—MORPHINE

HYDROXYZINE—HYDRALAZINE

IMIPENEM—OMNIPEN

LORABID—LEVBID

METRONIDAZOLE—METFORMIN

PEDIAPRED—PEDIAZOLE

PENICILLIN—PENICILLAMINE

PREDNISONE—PRILOSEC

PRIMACOR—PRIMAXIN

PULMOZYME—PULMICORT

SYNAGIS—SYNVISC

VANCOMYCIN—VECURONIUM

ZANTAC—XANAX

ZINACEF—ZITHROMAX

ZOFRAN—REGLAN

ZOFRAN—ZANTAC

ZOSYN—ZOFRAN
ZYRTEC—ZANTAC
ZYVOX—ZOVIRAX
ZYPREXA—ZYRTEC

The FDA estimates that 10 to 15 percent of medication errors are due to drug name confusion. Hopefully electronic prescribing as well as writing the indication for the treatment and both trade and generic names may reduce the number of errors made.

The color as well as the shape of the medication is only important if the trade name and same dosage of the drug is dispensed. When getting a generic medication even in the same dosage, the shape, color, and size can differ each time you refill the prescription. Therefore avoid describing medications by the shape size or color; this does not mean much even to a very well-trained and experienced pharmacist. This reminds me of a sweet eighty-six-year-old patient of mine who always tells me never to prescribe her any generic medication, much to the chagrin of her daughter who has to pay for all these trade names. I therefore append the abbreviations D.A.W. to all her prescriptions, which means "dispense as written" barring any substitutions by the pharmacist. Without these abbreviations on a prescription the pharmacist can use his or her discretion to dispense a generic in place of a trade name medication. A lot of people will swear certain generics do not work as well as some trade named medications. This is very possible because even though the active pharmacological ingredients are the same and the FDA demands a certain minimum percentage of this ingredient to be in the medicine, the medium with which the ingredients are mixed may differ, and therefore this may affect the availability of the medication after it is absorbed. Hence some people will swear that Motrin works better than ibuprofen or that Tylenol works better than acetaminophen. These are all individual preferences, just like some of us will pay more for name brands than store brands. As for me, I am cheap, so give me a generic every time!

Some drug companies write both the trade name and generic name of the medication on the bottle. This helps a great deal to prevent a lot of patient confusion. Medication that has two numbers separated by a forward slash (/) most likely consists of two separate medications; when listing the medications the dosage of the two halves must be correct. This is like macaroni and cheese; you can get the macaroni and cheese separate or together. It does not really matter because you can order them separately and eat them together; imagine paying a premium for macaroni and cheese together that far exceeds the cost of paying for each separately. But some insurance companies will not pay for a combination of medications. They will not pay for the patient's convenience of taking one pill instead of two or three separate ones.

While filling your prescription drugs, you have to shop around. In my experience the warehouse clubs provide the best deals on generics as well as some brand names. And no, you do not have to be a member to get your prescriptions filled at any warehouse club. In my experience pharmacies that offer the three- and four-dollar prescriptions for a month bank on the fact that you will fill the whole of your script with them, thereby affording them the opportunity to make a profit on the rest of the prescription. I just filled a six-month supply of metformin for a family member for about fifteen dollars! Tell me how you can beat that. In fact, some pharmacy chains now offer it for free.

For people without insurance, there are usually generic alternatives in most situations. Your physician will also be able to give you samples of medications that do not come in the generic form. I have a lot of patients who take advantage of prescription assistance programs of pharmaceutical companies. My office assists with filling of the paperwork, and the medication usually arrives at our office; we then pass it on to the patient. They usually give us a three- to six-month supply of the medicine.

Calling in Medications

Sometimes we as physicians are compelled by our patients to call in medications because they do not want to come in or want to avoid a co-pay. One of the reasons why we do not have a proliferation of call-in clinics is because medicine is a complex science. Seeing the patient is a part of the evaluation process. I had a patient who defected to my practice at one time all because her physician called in medications she wanted for an upper respiratory tract infection. It turned out that she had congestive heart failure, and of course, the cough and shortness of breath did not go away with a course of anti-biotics as well as antihistamines. If your doctor calls in medications for you and you do not feel better in three days, make an appointment to see him or her as soon as possible. Some medications cannot be called in, and a lot of physicians have stopped calling in narcotics to prevent abuse.

Pain Medications and Other Controlled Substances

This is a topic a lot of my colleagues avoid like the plague. Pain is a subjective feeling of discomfort that interferes with an individual's ability to function optimally. Unfortunately there is no "pain meter"; once an individual says he or she is in pain, as medical personnel we must believe him or her until proven otherwise. However, medical personnel are wary of the so-called "drug seekers" who show up at a physician's office for the first time on a Friday afternoon almost at the end of the day, ambulating with an antalgic gait and claiming they are allergic to all medications that could be used as alternatives for the control of their pain. They claim they are also intolerant of Motrin and all aspirin-like medications. Unfortunately the medical boards have turned physicians into some sort of detectives who have to ensure that there is proper documentation supporting the prescription of narcotic medication for that particular patient. Having been a Social Security disability examiner as well as an independent medical examiner, I can say with a degree of certainty that there are quite a few members of the public that put on quite a "show" when it comes to trying to prove they are in pain. Sometimes I have the opportunity of watching these people walk across the parking lot into my office, and I can see the marked difference in their gait while in the office compared to when they think no one is watching them.

There must be some sort of documentation of the cause of the pain, probably a radiological documentation or a subjective pain picture drawing as well as an attempt to document the level of pain. Some patients do not understand the pain level of 1–10 or the pain faces scale used to assess pain, 10 being the worst pain level ever possible. I have walked into a patient's room in the hospital while she was laughing and watching a Jerry Springer show and inquired about her pain; her reply was that it is a 10 out of 10! Come on now, you are not a medical provider, but would you believe this patient? On the contrary, you might even reduce the medicines she is on with the thought that she might be too euphoric!

We all know people who are in pain when we see them; however, in people who cannot talk on a ventilator or because of the advancement of their medical condition, physicians assess pain through several other methods including but not limited to behavior and facial grimaces as well as vital signs. We use this form of assessment a lot in hospice care to ensure patients are comfortable.

If you are in pain, let your physician know genuinely what the level of your pain or discomfort is. Cooperate while he or she tries to find out the cause of your pain. Do not suggest certain pain medications, but let your physician know what has not worked for you in the past. Also disclose what real allergies you have to certain medications. Bring copies of all your old records if you have any, as well as old prescription bottles if applicable. Do not try to bully the physician to prescribe a certain dose and frequency of medication because Dr. So-and-so has always written it for you that way. The physician who writes medications for you is responsible for his or her prescription as an independent qualified professional and can be questioned about prescribing habits at any time by the drug enforcement agency. A lot of pain medications are sold on the black market, and physicians are aware of and very wary of this. In fact, a lot of practices do not prescribe pain medications; the physicians refer the patients to their own primary care physician, like me, or to a pain management physician. Some of these physicians do not prescribe narcotics but try to alleviate a patient's pain by some other means, like steroid injections. The ones that do prescribe medications can be neurologists anesthesiologists or some orthopedic surgeons. These physicians usually ask patients to sign pain contracts and also subject patients to random urinary drug screens for controlled substances. In the event that the drug screen does not yield the substance being prescribed or yields some other substances not prescribed, the patient is "fired" from the program. I used to screen my patients' urine randomly, and I heard all sorts of stories; some patients were prescribed opiates but marijuana was found in their urine because the neighbor downstairs is a habitual marijuana smoker and the smoke filtered through the floorboards!

Safeguard your narcotic prescriptions and do not let them get lost or stolen. I have had to ask for a police report in order to replace a patient's narcotic prescription. Also ensure that your medications will last the weekend or for the period you are out of town. I and the other solo internists that cross cover each other have agreed that we will not call in narcotic pain medications, especially on the weekends for patients we have never seen. This is a way to prevent abuse; one of my colleagues had an employee of his calling in narcotics under fictitious names and selling them on the street. He was investigated by the DEA, but it was obvious after a short period that it was his employee calling in the medications. I have also had patients call in controlled medications for themselves, and very smart pharmacists have caught on to this because they personally know the prescribing habits of local physicians as well as some of their staff. When taking narcotics from one physician, do not shop for other physicians that will prescribe other narcotics for you or go to other pharmacies because your health insurance company will find out and may put you on a "pharmacy lockdown" program whereby you can only fill your prescriptions at one pharmacy.

Recently a local pharmacist called me to alert me that some individual had made prescription pads with the name of my practice and were trying to fill narcotics at his pharmacy. I asked him to fax me the scripts, which were made out to individuals who are not even patients in my practice on prescription pads that were obviously forged. I had to make an unscheduled visit to the police station to report this. In my opinion controlled substances should be under a tighter regulation with a numbered duplicated prescription for each physician so that there can be tracking of each script. This will make it easy to reconcile and audit each doctor's script.

When my practice initiated the rule that we would only provide written scripts for all controlled substances, we got some resistance from our clients; even though we gave them several months' notice, some of them still insisted that they were unaware of our new policy. I happened to be on call for myself one night when I received a call through my answering service about a patient of mine who was suffering from abdominal pains. She happened to be well-known to me, and as soon as I returned her call she expressed profound gratitude that I had returned the call and also that I was on call for myself. She went on to describe her symptoms of abdominal pain as well as a low-grade fever, which had started a couple of hours earlier and was associated with some vomiting. She said it was initially around her umbilicus and then settled in her groin area. She went on to conclude that it was her "kidney stones" acting up again and I should oblige her by calling in some antibiotics and her usual pain medicines, and she would see me in the morning. I carefully explained to her that I would be doing her a great disservice by calling in what she requested. I further said I was suspicious that something else was going on and I recommended she go to the emergency room to be evaluated.

She was not happy! She called me every name in the book and told me she would be in the emergency room "all night" just because her primary doctor refused to do what was right. I told her to call her urologist if he would do what she wanted but that I suspected something else was going on. She went on to say that was a lame excuse and I was saying so only because I did not want to do what she wanted. She hung up the phone, but not before I told her I insisted she go to the closest emergency room. When I hung up the phone I called the emergency room closest to her residence and talked to the charge nurse to be expecting a very unhappy patient in triage soon. About an hour later I got a call from one of the emergency room physicians who told me he had carried out a CT scan of her abdomen; she had an acute appendix and was on the way to the operating room! I thanked him and asked to be informed of her room number. The next morning when I saw her she was very apologetic, saying that I had saved her life. She said after she hung up the phone the pain got really bad, and she then realized it could not be her usual kidney stones and called the ambulance for transportation to the hospital. She had some family members in the room, and they were all very grateful. I shared this story with my other colleagues, and it further buttressed our decision never to call in pain medications. She is still my patient today, and she never fails to tell anyone who sits beside her in my waiting room the story of how I saved her life. By the way, the surgeon told me she was just in time because her appendix looked like it would have ruptured at any moment!

When moving from one state to another, if you are on heavy duty pain medications, have your physician contact a local doctor in the city you are planning to move to and give him or her a physician-to-physician report. All your records should accompany you to the first visit of this new physician. I have had this done a couple of times, and it saved patients a lot of hassle; I was able to provide a soft landing, and even though I am not a pain physician I was able to at least refill the medications and redirect them to pain clinics that are still caring for them today.

Another common group of controlled substances asked for by most people is medications for "nerves." When people ask about this they are referring to a very popular medication that is also sold on the streets, and when they are offered anything but that medicine they usually decline. Someone with bad nerves needs to see a psychiatrist, but most people just want this group of medications, which could be habit forming, requiring higher and higher doses of the same drug to achieve the same effects. The medications are also not expected to be discontinued abruptly because this can lead to withdrawal symptoms or seizures in some cases.

Unfortunately, some health care workers including nurses and doctors have been caught diverting medications for patients to themselves or their family and friends. If you or a family member is addicted to pain medications or other habit-forming medicines, help is available. Please discuss this with your physician today before the problem gets out of hand. This may be in the form of a pain medication or nerve pill, an opioid-containing cough mixture, a habit-forming muscle relaxant, or sleeping medications, among others. Be your brothers' keepers and watch out for your friends, coworkers, and associates. When people empha-size the need for certain medicines or have to take more and more of the same medication to achieve the same effect, they are probably dependent or addicted to the medication in question.

CHAPTER 4

Medical and Surgical Specialties

Some people mistake me as an internist for being an "internal doctor" meaning that I should be taking care of everything on the inside. Patients usually better understand me when I say I am a primary care physician. I am in a medical specialty, which means I diagnose and treat people with medicines. Internists are not trained to operate, although they may do incision and drainage of small abscesses and boils, and they can put in some special intravenous lines or put a tube down the throat to place a patient on a ventilator. Depending on where they are practicing and the availability of a subspecialist, internists may be called upon to increase their level of skill by further training. For instance, they may perform colonoscopies, stress tests, or esophagogastroduodenoscopy—looking into the esophagus and stomach—on some patients.

Medical specialties are generally non-operating specialties. Surgical specialties operate on people after they are either put to sleep completely or partially by an anesthesiologist or the area being operated on is completely numbed, as is done in a spinal or regional block. There are other numerous career choices for a recent internal medicine graduate, including research, joining the armed forces or joining a teaching hospital for an academic career. Some people decide they want to be specialists after completing internal medicine; this means they have to go back for one to three more years to become a cardiologist, rheumatologist, endocrinologist, pulmonologist and critical care specialist, nephrologist, gastroenterologist, or to specialize in hematology, oncology, infectious diseases, radiation oncology, hospice and palliative medicine, geriatrics, or toxicology.

After becoming a cardiologist you can decide to be an interventionalist, an echocardiographer, or an electrophysiologist. These need additional training of two to three years. Remember these are all "medical" specialties and do not operate. They carry out sophisticated procedures that resemble surgery to the layperson but are not considered so in the medical community. For instance, the interventionalist may go through a patient's groin or arm to perform a balloon angioplasty or stent placement on a patient's heart. Nowadays they can also open up blocked vessels in patient's lower extremities. An echocardiographer, also called a noninvasive cardiologist, may be able to do three-dimensional echography or look at an MRI of the heart as well as interpret calcium scoring tests. An electrophysiologist also performs procedures on the heart, like investigating an irregular heartbeat in order to find out why a patient has it and how to possibly correct it. Electrophysiologists sometimes refer to themselves as the electricians of the heart, while interventionists are sometimes called the plumbers of the heart.

Pulmonologists treat everything to do with the lungs, sleep apnea, and placing people on breathing machines. Some of them are certified in sleep medicine as well. The gastroenterologist deals with the whole of the gastrointestinal tract from the mouth to the anus and also the liver, gall bladder, and pancreas. The nephrologist deals with the kidneys—dialysis, etc.—while the rheumatologist deals with the disorders of muscle, bones, and joints. The endocrinologist deals with disorders of diabetes, bones, thyroid, reproduction, and all endocrine glands. The hematologist/oncologist deals with blood disorders and cancer. The infectious disease specialist deals with infections, and the toxicologist deals with poisons, toxins, and drug overdoses.

In teaching hospitals you see a lot of sub specialization; for instance you might see an endocrinologist that deals mostly with the thyroid gland or a gastroenterologist whose research interest is gastric ulcers. There are varied combinations of the above specialists. For instance, you may have a physician do nephrology and critical care. These are all medical specialties; none of these specialists operate on patients, although they have similar surgical counterparts. For instance, the primary care physician or internist has an equivalent in the general surgeon who can operate on appendixes, colons, and gallbladders. The cardiologist's surgical counterpart is the cardiothoracic surgeon, who carries out bypass surgery on the heart. This same surgeon can operate on the lungs to remove tumors. The gastroenterologist might refer to a colorectal surgeon, while a rheumatologist has an orthopedic surgeon as a surgical counterpart. The nephrologist's most equivalent surgical counterpart is the urologist, who takes care of kidney stones as well as prostate issues, to mention a few. The hematologist/oncologist has a surgical oncologist as a counterpart. Again, you can have combinations of any of the surgical specialties; for instance, there are oncology surgeons that deal with the surgical excision of tumors. In some cases depending on the complexity of the case you can have an urologist operate with a colorectal surgeon to remove a kidney mass that has involved the colon as well. There are other surgical combinations like an uro-gynecologist. This is a gynecologist and urologist in one, and these highly trained individuals specialize in treating women with pelvic floor issues and other ailments.

All the medical specialties above are considered to be members of the department of medicine. There is another specialty that is also considered a member of the department but has not completed a full internal medicine specialty. The neurologist rotates through the department but has a special residency program, and some are now being combined with psychiatry. The neurologist deals with disorders of the brain and the nervous system, which include strokes, seizures, headaches, and multiple sclerosis as well as disorders of the muscle and nerves. They are also trained to perform tests like nerve conduction studies. The surgical component is the neurosurgeon, who carries out operations on the brain as well as the nervous system. These individuals can remove tumors from the brain and also operate on slipped discs in the spine.

Family practitioners are also members of the department of medicine, and they have been trained in taking care of adults (internists), kids (pediatricians), and pregnant women (obstetricians), as well as minor surgical problems. Generally they end up practicing mostly pediatrics as well as internal medicine. A lot of them end up dropping the surgical specialties like obstetrics, gynecology, and minor surgical procedures because of various reasons including but not limited to high malpractice premiums.

There are some other specialties that are sort of a medical and a surgical specialty combined. The ones that come easily to mind are ophthalmologists as well as dermatologists. These specialties are basically surgical, but they can function as medical specialties as well. Podiatrists are also surgeons and carry out surgeries on the ankle and feet.

Psychiatrists are a separate specialty that are not members of the department of medicine but are very closely linked. Internists can treat minor psychiatric problems, which are quickly referred to a psychiatrist when expert care is needed. A lot of patients are quickly on the defensive when told they are being referred to a psychiatrist. "So you think I'm crazy" or "I am not crazy" is the response I always expect. My response is always that the amount of expertise needed to resolve whatever the patient's problem is exceeds my training, and this usually calms the patient down.

Physician assistants and nurse practitioners have become very important members of the health-care delivery team. They can be attached to any specialty and usually practice under the license of a board-certified physician. In the state of Georgia, the physician assistant (PA) can prescribe controlled substances while nurse practitioners (NP) cannot. They usually have to discuss your case with a physician, who has to sign off on it. These highly trained individuals work from the emergency room to the operating room as well as in doctors' offices. If your preference is to see a physician in the office, let your primary care physician know that. I have had several patients show up in my practice from another office with a main complaint being that they never saw a physician and were unhappy with their care. PAs and NPs, while highly trained professionals who definitely have a role in the health-care delivery system, may not be the best option for a patient with multiple medical problems.

A physician assistant is different from a medical assistant who is usually seen in a doctor's office. The physician assistant is a college graduate and has a more detailed training than a medical assistant, who is trained for about twelve to eighteen months depending on the state and the program. A lot of patients refer to medical assistants in the office as nurses, but they are not. A lot of physician offices employ nurses who work as supervisors to medical assistants, who are the equivalent of hospital techs in the office. They have the basic knowledge of running either the front office or the back office for the doctor, and the longer they are part of an office the more experience they have.

Another important group of paramedical professionals mostly in the hospital setting are patient care technicians and phlebotomists. These individuals, also called the "techs," carry out a lot of procedures ordered by doctors or nurses. They can draw blood, do electrocardiograms, and carry out pulmonary function tests among a long list of responsibilities. Also called "techs" are the individuals who carry out ultrasounds and other tests ordered by the physician. They carry out the technical portion, and the interpretation is done by the physician in that subspecialty. For instance, a cardiologist can order an echocardiogram, which I also refer to as an ultrasound of the heart, so people have an idea of what I am talking about. After the test has been done by the tech, the doctor reviews the film and writes a report. In some emergencies and in teaching hospitals the cardiologist in training or the actual cardiologist might have to do the test if the tech is not available for some reason or the other. It is felt to be more cost efficient for the tech to carry out the test instead of the cardiologist utilizing time in this way when it could be better spent doing other things that require specific skill and expertise.

A lot of patients usually put techs under enormous pressure by asking what they see. When people are ill, there is a certain amount of anxiety that accompanies the sickness, and therefore they are looking for information wherever it may be found. Do not ask a tech for an interpretation of your test; the physician still has to review the films and issue a final report. Most technicians are very experienced and can pretty much tell you what the interpretation of the test is, but in some circumstances they are wrong.

It is very important that you know exactly who your pri mary doctor wants you to see. For instance, I had a patien who was seeing a nephrologist for his chronic kidney dis ease, and then he developed an abnormal prostate test so I asked him to see an urologist. He verbalized understand ing, I made the appointment for him and gave him the nec essary information, and I emphasized the importance o seeing this doctor so that he could possibly do a biopsy to confirm or discard my suspicion. I saw the patient a month later and inquired about the urology consultation; he said he did not bother to see the one I sent him to because he was already seeing one. When I asked who he was seeing he gave me the name of a nephrologist! I quickly explained the difference and again urged him to see the urologist as soon as possible. He did, and thank God his prostate biopsy was negative.

Nurses

Since we are on the topic of professional designations, it is now appropriate to talk a bit about nurses. These are among the most selfless and caring professionals I know. It is a tough profession both while schooling and working. I know this firsthand because my sister-in law is a nurse. Any-one who decides to be a nurse because of the financial rewards will not last long because it is physically and men-tally demanding. There are a lot of other professionals in the health-care field—nursing aides, nursing assistants, nutri-tion aides, and staff of the environmental services depart-ment—who would love to be referred to as nurses or tell their relatives they are nurses or because they have assisted nurses for several years believe they are now equivalent to nurses. On several occasions I have been asked by family members to discuss the clinical status of a family member with another family member who is a "nurse." In many instances the family depends on this "nurse" for decision making. After one second talking to this nurse I usually find him or her grossly deficient of the basic knowledge needed to follow and interpret the medical facts associated with the ill family member. I hear things like the family is not going to give consent for a certain invasive test that will shed more light on the situation just because these people do not want to expose their ignorance about medical matters. I encourage all families who believe they have a nurse as a family member to please confirm that that individual is indeed a licensed practical nurse—LPN—or a registered nurse—RN.

A lot of nurses have specializations just like physicians do. Nurses who have worked in a neonatal unit all their lives cannot tell you much about medications used to treat diabetes and hypertension in adults, just like I will need some guidance from a nurse when I enter a neonatal intensive care unit. We all should resist obtaining advice from people who are not professionally qualified to do so and lack the expertise and or the education. There is no way we can turn an office bookkeeper into a financial planner. We should also desist from getting medical advice from our neighbors. When my patients tell me about suggestions from their neighbor, I usually ask what the neighbor's specialty is, and if the response is that the neighbor is not a physician the point is usually made. Believe me, I am not discarding every piece of information that is presented to me. I listen and then explain why this situation is different. For example, let's take a seemingly simple medical problem like a headache. There is an International Society of Headaches! These are people who come from all over the world to discuss headaches, which reveals that this single symptom is even more complex than anyone can imagine; therefore the chances that headaches between neighbors could be due to exactly the same cause is very slim.

Second opinions are always welcome in medicine, but please ensure that you are comparing apples to apples. Ensure that whomever you want to ask for a second opinion is of at least the same qualifications as the professional offering a certain treatment option. A good source of information is your primary care physician. I have an elderly male patient, whom I have been taking care of for several years, with a benign growth in the base of his brain that is being followed by a multidisciplinary group of physicians as well as a neurosurgeon. Recently his sight started to deteriorate, and all the subspecialists he was seeing recommended surgery. He told all of them he would not consider it unless I agreed as well. It had been a while since I reviewed that particular surgery, so I carried out an extensive review of the literature and eventually agreed with all his specialists because his vision was failing, affecting his ability to drive and hence his independence. My patient relied on me for his decision but should have asked another neurosurgeon for his opinion. He did well postoperatively and is back to his usual preoperative functional status.

Surgeries

At some point in most people's life they will be faced with the decision of whether or not to have surgery. When the surgery is an emergent one, there is no option. The decision is simple, you would think; however, some individuals request more time to think about the surgery. For instance, I admitted a highly functional eighty-year-old woman who had her intestines twisted up on themselves, requiring urgent surgery. Time was of the essence because part of her bowels could die and no longer be viable. This lady refused even though all members of her family knew she needed the surgery, and we all tried to impress on her the urgency in the matter. She eventually agreed, and according to the surgeon he was able to preserve the viability of the colon in the nick of time or she would have ended up with a colostomy—a stool bag—and possibly other postoperative complications.

An elective surgery, however, is one that can wait for a period of time, for instance, a small reducible hernia or cosmetic surgery. The surgeon will inform you of the risks and benefits as well as alternatives to the procedure. General surgical risks include bleeding, infection, and wound breakdown, loss of proper function of the operated anatomic body part, and chronic pain as well as scars. Though all might go well before, during, and after the operation, complications can still occur. Respiratory failure or the inability to come off the ventilator after surgery may occur if general anesthesia is utilized. In some situations other means of anesthesia are used to reduce the complications of general anesthesia. These options include epidurals—very common for childbirth—regional anesthesia, and nerve blocks. These are not options for certain types of surgeries, and it requires an anesthesiologist as well as a surgeon to decide on appropriate alternatives.

Whenever elective surgery is planned, generally speaking all blood thinners should be stopped, as well as all aspirin-like products and non-steroidal anti-inflammatory medications, which are mostly over-the-counter medications. For elective surgeries, you can actually donate your own blood over a period of time so that your blood can be reinfused into your body if necessary during or after surgery. Postoperatively you will be sent to the recovery room and then admitted to hospital for an overnight stay if necessary. Antibiotics are usually given before surgery to reduce the risk of postoperative infections. Some individuals with certain heart conditions require antibiotics before simple things like deep cleaning of their teeth to prevent fatal infections of the heart valves.

Generally speaking we are able to predict the kind of complications expected in different surgeries and in all elective surgeries in patients over thirty-five years of age, as well as in those with multiple medical problems. The surgeon sends a patient to his or her primary care doctor for a surgical clearance. The primary care doctor in turn carries out a preoperative risk assessment on the patient based on the type of surgery, the patient's history, and the outcome of certain tests. In some cases we have to send the patient to the cardiologist for further testing. At the end we determine if the individual is low, intermediate, or high risk. If we determine the individual is too high risk for the procedure and there is no way to reduce this risk, we recommend against the surgery.

Some people go doctor shopping to find a doctor that will clear them for the surgery. We all remember the case of the mother of a Hollywood superstar who died after cosmetic surgery; some physicians came out later to say they would not have cleared her for the surgery because she was too high risk, but the surgery was done anyway. Low risk, however, does not mean that once a person is cleared for surgery the operation must go well without complications. It only means that there are very minimal untoward possibilities of complications following surgery, and efforts will of course be made to further reduce the risks of the surgery. A car can go through a rigorous one-hundred-point inspection and still end up having problems on the freeway. Surgery of any kind is still a risk, period. The risk reduces with the maximization of the health of the individual before surgery.

In some individuals we may advice cessation of tobacco consumption or some weight loss as well as moderate exercise, all of which help to reduce postoperative morbidity and mortality. The risk of surgery is also affected by the *type* of surgery. Obviously brain, heart, and vascular surgery carry the greatest risks. The surgeon who plans to operate also is a factor in the outcome of the operation. Obviously any surgeon who has performed several of the procedures in question with minimal complications is likely to be able to perform another one with minimal risk. A surgical subspecialist who spends most of his or her career removing gall bladders is likely to be able to remove another one with eyes closed. Asking me to remove a gall bladder would take an act of God because the last time I did one was about twenty-five years ago during my internship.

Another factor is the facility where the surgery is to take place. Everything can be perfect, but if the facility lacks the appropriate and up-to-date equipment as well as staff, then the patient is in trouble. When the morbidity and mortality from bariatric surgery were higher than acceptable, the Centers for Medicare Services designated some facilities as centers of excellence for bariatric surgery.

Some families still refuse emergency surgeries. I have had a few patients in hospital with hip fractures whose families refused to let them to have surgery, their reasoning being that they did not think the patient would pull through the surgery. This subjects the patient to excruciating discomfort as well as a bedridden lifestyle. Even close to the end of life, surgery may be contemplated in order to reduce the amount of pain and suffering, so-called palliative surgery. In summary, for emergent surgery we pretty much do not have a choice; the surgery will have to be done, and the medical doctor—internist—will do his or her best to ensure that the risk of complications post-surgery is reduced to the barest minimum. As for elective surgery, please ensure you see your internist as well as any other specialist that he or she might recommend. In this situation there is plenty of time to reduce risk and maximize recovery. Always ask your internist for a referral and get a second opinion if you are not happy with the surgeon you have; and remember, a breast reduction is no emergency and we can always wait to have it done properly.

A lot of Americans are now traveling overseas for elective surgeries—the so-called "medical tourism." I recently attended a conference during which the presenter was talking about kidney transplants being done on patients in developing countries by physicians in Asia. The presentation showed what most people suspect: some of the facilities where the operations occurred were far below the standards in the United States, and also the organs transplanted were a poor match. To add insult to injury, the patients were usually bundled onto a plane back to their countries of origin at the early stages of rejection. The take-home message from the presenter was obvious; whenever medical tourism is being considered, please involve your physician so he or she can recommend reputable surgeons as well as facilities to you overseas. Remember that these places are not subject to the same standard of care as in the United States. You might even be able to locate an American Board Certified surgeon to operate in a foreign country.

CHAPTER 5

Hospital Admissions

There are several ways to get admitted into a hospital. One of the most common is when you are sentenced to hospital through the emergency room. The emergency room was set up to take care of emergencies regardless of the ability to pay and national origin. As long as you are on the soil of the United States, when you step into the emergency room with a real emergency, you will be taken care of. The emergency room physicians will diagnose and treat you on the spot. They will order the appropriate tests and arrive at a diagnosis so as to determine if you need to be in the hospital or not. The most important duty of emergency room physicians is to determine the severity of the illness you present with and if you really need to be in hospital or can be discharged home.

Medicine is highly complicated, and any individual can have a serious medical problem that will present with a mild symptom. A classic example of this is a heart attack presenting as a pain in the jaw. This actually happened to a physician at one of the hospitals where I practice. He started having jaw pain while in the physicians lounge and was quickly suspected to be having a heart attack by another physician present, who insisted he go to the emergency room, where he ended up having the blocked artery opened within a short period of time. As expected he is profoundly grateful to the physician who suspected he was having a heart attack.

At the other end of the spectrum, patients can have what they see as a very serious medical condition being treated with levity in the emergency room. An example is back pain, which is chronic in most people—their back just goes out. In the emergency room after ensuring that the back pain is not due to a neurological emergency, the patient is sent home much to his or her surprise. The physicians in the emergency room are under an enormous amount of pressure to see as many people as possible within a short period of time. In addition to this, they have to be able to decide if a patient has a life-threatening illness or not. They are held to very high standards and are penalized very heavily for any mistakes; the rate they are sued is higher than in a lot of other medical specialties.

Most of the results obtained in the emergency room are preliminary reports. There are some blood tests that are available almost immediately, while others like blood cultures do not become available for three to four days. It is of extreme importance to leave the correct contact information so that if results are abnormal you can be contacted. A lot of people with no health insurance go to the emergency room and give a lot of false information because they do not want the billing department to be able to get a hold of them. Yes, they even use fake Social Security numbers.

Some radiological reports are also preliminary, and the emergency room physician gives an initial impression, which the radiologist either confirms or gives a different opinion. A lot of patients have been asked to follow up in my office from the emergency room for "pneumonia." On arrival in my office the official report does not state "pneumonia," and the patient ends up being upset because he was told he has pneumonia from the emergency room. The patient is already feeling better, and the diagnosis probably was "bronchitis" but the treatment for pneumonia helped the patient get better.

Once the emergency room physician completes an assessment on a patient and decides if the patient needs to be admitted, the patient is then asked for the information of whomever he or she sees for this particular problem. An example is if a patient has an established cardiologist and comes in with a heart attack; then the cardiologist will be called to facilitate the admission process. However, if the cardiologist in question does not have admitting privileges in that hospital, the cardiologist may be given the option of asking another cardiologist to admit the patient. In the absence of a cardiologist willing to facilitate the admission process, there are always physicians of various specialties on call to admit patients who have no physician in that hospital. This issue, to me, is very important. A lot of patients choose physicians who live a long way from home because of the quality of care they feel that physician renders them. In an emergency room situation, such patients would most likely be admitted by physicians who hardly know them because a lot of physicians generally have admission privileges in hospitals close to where their offices are or where they live. Some hospitals even have stipulated in their bylaws the number of miles away from the office or home each physician is allowed to commute. I have heard that a member of hospital staff will actually drive the distance to determine if it is within the acceptable limits. In the event that the patient does not have a "local" physician then one will be assigned.

If family members of the patient have been admitted in the same hospital and experienced excellent care in the hands of a certain physician, the patient may ask for that physician, who then has the option of accepting treatment responsibility. The physician requested may not be on call that particular day, so his or her covering colleague will be the one to care for the patient. The only physician under any obligation to accept a patient from the emergency room is the physician on call, who usually cannot refuse a patient unless the physician is not on the patient's insurance plan and there is an alternative physician willing to take over the care of this patient. Of course, this is a moot point if we are talking about an emergency. Some health maintenance organizations actually dictate who the admitting physicians can be out of their "panel" of physicians. In some cases the HMOs allow you to admit a patient, and after twenty-four to forty-eight hours they start to call the physician to transfer care to one of their "panel" physicians.

So you have stayed in the emergency room for hours and the emergency room physicians as well as the admitting physician actually have discussed your case. They might agree to run a few more tests in the emergency room in order to confirm the diagnosis or to decide on whether you can be discharged. The take-home message here is that you never want to be an "interesting" case. I always hope that my friends, family members and I are boring, run-of-the-mill cases whenever we are sentenced to a hospital!

If you are to be admitted, the admitting physician gives orders to a nurse or in some small emergency rooms the ER physician. At the point orders are given, you are no longer under the care of the ER physician unless you develop an emergency in the ER while awaiting your bed and your admitting physician is not around. The admitting physician stipulates a lot of things regarding your admission; for example, pain medications, intravenous fluids, and further investigations that he or she feels you are likely to need. In some cases the admitting physician will be in the hospital at the time of your admission, and you will get to see him or her that day or night. Nowadays a lot of hospitals have hospitalists on staff that are doctors who carry out only hospital care. They run in shifts like nurses, and they do not have offices outside of the hospital so no matter how much you love your hospitalist he or she cannot take care of you in the office. A lot of physicians have stopped admitting their own patients in the hospital and have deferred the care of their patients to hospitalists. Actually, physicians like me who combine office and hospital practices are a dying breed.

The future is that physicians either stay in the hospital *or* the office but not both. Now there are even various specialists who are hospitalists; for instance, there are neurology hospitalists as well as intensive care specialists that are hospitalists; any specialty can be a hospitalist. In fact, the hospitalist movement is now extending to surgical specialties like general surgery.

So you are admitted by a physician who will henceforth be known as your admitting or attending physician; usually his or her name will be on the arm band that you wear while in the hospital. This attending physician is primarily responsible for your care in the hospital and can ask for the help of any subspecialist to manage your case. Again, before this happens you will be asked if you have any preference; most patients leave the choice of the specialist up to whoever their attending physician is. So the physician is like the project manager who assembles a team of subcontractors to build a house or carry out a project for the client, in this case the patient.

During your hospitalization you will come across numerous health-care providers; it is almost impossible to keep track of everyone. You have the certified nursing assistants who usually take your vital signs and generally assist your nurse to take care of your needs. Sometimes they are called patient care technicians. Your nurse could be a licensed practical nurse (LPN) or a registered nurse (RN). Depending on the hospital, certain levels of nurses are excluded from certain levels of care. You will also come into contact with various other professionals which may include but are not limited to dietitians, wound care nurses, pharmacists, therapists (both speech and occupational as well as physical), and finally a case manager to plan your discharge.

Should you have any complaints during your hospitalization you can report to the charge nurse or the nurse supervisor, who will direct you to the appropriate person. The charge nurse usually handles nursing and other administrative complaints while physician complaints should be directed to the hospitalist medical director if you are being cared for by the hospitalist, or the chief of the Department of Medicine if the practitioner is a private physician.

Most physicians are independent contractors apart from the hospitalists who are employed by companies that have a contract with the hospitals or are employed directly by the hospital. If something goes wrong while you are in the hospital and you do not like your doctor, you can request a change; but once this happens other physicians may be wary of you. You can always ask for a second opinion, especially if a surgical remedy is recommended. You can also always ask to have your nurse changed if you feel there are lapses in care or you just do not trust him or her. The hospital cannot fire a physician whom it does not employ; it can, however, suspend the physician's privileges after due process and investigations. This can become very messy in some cases and has resulted in lawsuits between hospitals and physicians whenever the case cannot be settled amicably.

It is important that your next of kin has a functioning phone number that will be placed on your chart. I say *functioning* because time and time again I have had to call the next of kin only to find out that the phone has been disconnected. I usually have to solicit the help of a social worker to find the next of kin. These days with the privacy laws, health-care workers cannot discuss any part of your illness with any member of your family without your permission. But everyone needs a health-care advocate to understand why they are being admitted and what tests will be run. When you are sick and in a strange environment, fear and anxiety play a big role, and therefore patients often hear what is being said but do not understand or digest it. I have admitted several very intelligent patients who ask me every day on rounds, "So, Doc, what do you say is wrong with me?" I explain again for the umpteenth time why they are in the hospital and what the plan is. Sometimes, however, it is the relative who is under stress and does not understand what is being said. I often hear complaints like "No one is telling us what's going on. They take blood every day but no one has told us any results." The person who hears this the most is the nurse caring for the patient, so what I do in some cases is to take the nurse into the room with me on my first contact with the patient and family to explain all that we know so far about the patient's illness.

Please delegate only one family member as the spokesperson. This should be the person all other family members call to get information from and also to relay questions that should be asked from the doctor. You can imagine people with a dozen family members calling from all over the country asking about the patient's progress. Choosing one allows for a seamless flow of information through the same individual thereby avoiding any confusion in the information obtained and relayed. It is mutually beneficial to both physician and patient to have one representative be the intermediary between the family and the physician. In certain special situations there can be a backup relative designated just in case the main contact cannot be located.

So it is much better to have one representative per patient that is easily reachable. The relative is "on call" day and night as long as the family member is still in hospital because the doctor may want to call him or her at any time to discuss a change in status and to make urgent decisions regarding the direction of care. I try to give an update in person to the relative at least once in two days. However, whenever there is a major setback or major improvement, or when we have to carry out invasive procedures or transfuse patients with blood, I usually call.

Remember, being in the hospital is very stressful to the patient as well as all the family members. Ensure you know what is going on at every stage of your care; be firm, polite, and persistent in your wishes, but don't go overboard like I have seen some people do. Some families have a family member in the room running shifts at all times recording the time each individual comes in what their names are and what they did to the patients. Some even keep a log of how often their family member, who is unable to move for whatever reason, gets turned while in bed. The classic example I have seen is the family of a hospitalized patient with a video camera in a conspicuous place in the patient's room recording all the events that take place! In this situation the health-care providers I am sure were playing to the gallery; I am certain that being pleasant and firm to the health-care team would yield better results than a video camera!

The Discharge Process

Hopefully things went well during your hospitalization and you get to be discharged. Most hospitals have discharge planners who take care of the discharge process. These people are also referred to as case managers, and most of them have a nursing background. There are several possibilities after your hospitalization. The best is that you are discharged home. You might need various things at home like a hospital bed, a bedside commode, oxygen, etc., some of which are called durable medical equipment or DME for short. The case manager liaises with your doctor to get a home care company to deliver all these items. Sometimes you may qualify for home physical therapy or home health care, e.g., for a nurse to come out to your house to check your blood pressure or blood sugar or both. You will be given explicit discharge instructions on your discharge papers. Please have your designated family health-care advocate to be present at the discharge if possible. This is where a lot of errors occur, so you should be very clear as to what is expected of you. You want to know the answer to the following questions from your physician before going home.

- What was my diagnosis?
- Is it life threatening?
- Have I been cured or it is a chronic disease that I will have for the rest of my life?
- What caused it and how can I prevent future episodes of the illness?
- Do I have dietary restrictions?
- What warning signs of reoccurrence should I look out for?
- Are my kids or relatives at any risk?
- When do I go back to work?
- Which doctor is it most important for me to see first as a follow-up?
- How many doctors do I need to see as a follow-up to my illness?
- Whom do I call if I have questions?
- How does my primary care physician get all the records from the hospital?
- I have no insurance; what is my best bet for continued care?
- Do I need any further tests on discharge?

You may need to be discharged to a nursing home as a bridge to finally going home. Your family members will have to agree in consultation with you which one they choose. I have heard and seen family members decide beforehand they want a particular nursing home or rehabilitation center and will not settle for anything else, even if their preferred nursing home is full or is not approved by their insurance company. Another discharge option is hospice care, either inpatient or outpatient. This one is very tricky, and usually people are admitted to an inpatient hospice for symptom management or if they are actively dying. But the hospice does not only serve the people who are actively dying, but they can also assist home hospice cases when there is caregiver breakdown or for respite or for some sort of symptom control. The clients at home are visited by physicians and nurses as well as nursing aides. In fact, the home hospice clients probably have the best home care, and rightly so which even the acutely ill do not benefit from.

Sometimes family members believe that transfer to hospice means the patient will die there; they are later disappointed when their loved one's symptoms have stabilized and the hospice is talking about discharge planning. I usually hear relatives say that they were informed in the hospital that the patient could stay in the hospice facility for the rest of their lives. Generally speaking the only people who stay in hospice till the end of life are people who are actively dying or rapidly declining in their physical or functional status.

Another discharge possibility is a long-term acute care hospital also known as LTAC. This concept is relatively new, and a lot of people are confused about it. The area I practice in the South Metro Atlanta has some LTACs that actually rent a floor in a community hospital. A lot of patients are confused about this, and I always hear them say they would prefer to stay where they are rather than move to another floor of the hospital. This brings me to insurance companies and length of stay issues. When a patient is admitted in hospital, the insurance company keeps tabs on the patient and calls the case manager and or the attending physician to get an update on the patient regularly. They have certain average lengths of stay for certain illnesses; for instance, an admission for pneumonia should be four to five days. Should the patient stay longer, the hospital does not get paid for the extended stay unless it can prove that the patient had a complication of the pneumonia. The companies use patient data like lab work, X-rays, etc., but they do not see the patient. Herein comes the conflict sometimes. The patient can look awful and the numbers look good and the insurance company begins to deny payment. The LTACS came into being as a win-win situation for the insurance companies as well as patients. For instance, if a patient needs antibiotics to be given through the vein for six weeks for the treatment of an infection, the LTAC can be a choice instead of the patient going home, especially if other services like wound care are needed. If a patient needs more time to be weaned off a ventilator, then the LTAC is the place. These places are actually *hospitals*.

Other options in the discharge process include a rehabilitation center, a personal care home, or a shelter. I have actually witnessed a hospital buy a plane ticket for an illegal immigrant back to his country of origin after being cured because it was the safest discharge plan for that patient at that point in time. A transfer to a different hospital is another discharge option. This may occur if a procedure that is needed cannot be carried out in the hospital the patient is admitted to; for instance, if bypass surgery is needed, a tertiary hospital may be required to accept the patient.

It is part of the hospital's responsibility to provide a safe discharge plan. The hospital may be found liable if the discharge plan is not considered safe. An example is a bed-ridden, demented patient being sent back home to live by himself; this is obviously not a safe discharge plan. In many cases there is a conflict in what the family feels is safe and what the health-care team thinks. In the same situation I stated above, the patient may have an elderly wife who gets around with a walker who insists on taking him home to care for him alone. It is clearly impossible for her to care for him safely. She even has difficulty caring for herself! The hospital discharge team tries to accommodate the wishes of the family, but this is not possible all the time and compromises have to be made.

Living Will

It is virtually routine now that everyone admitted into the hospital is asked about a living will and what their wishes are if their heart should suddenly stop. This question sounds scary. "Is it that serious?" is the question I hear patients ask. In medicine, because a lot of things are unpredictable and anything can happen at any time, we like to be prepared for the worst. I have admitted so many people whom I feel are going to make it, and they take a turn for the worse and die. I have also admitted patients that are in extremis when they come in but end up walking out of the hospital and even come back to say hello to everyone on a victory lap.

The living will is a document that states how you want to be treated when you are seriously ill. It talks about medical, personal, emotional, physical, and spiritual needs. It also talks about whom you want to make health-care decisions for you in case you are not able to. There are generally five wishes in a living will. These five wishes are accepted in most of the states in the US. The living will format was created by the American Bar Association's Commission on Law and Aging, and it is basic and easy to use. I will briefly mention these wishes and common errors that are made surrounding them.

The first is to choose a person as your health-care agent. This person must know you very well and understand what your health-care wishes are. This individual must also have the time and be willing to be your health-care advocate if the need arises. Most people chose a spouse or family member, but when the chips are down immediate family members are often too emotional to make the right decisions. For example, some patients I have known elect not to be fed when they are terminally ill. Some family members may deem this to be inhumane, and they have a hard time implementing the wishes of the sick family member even though several studies have failed to show a survival advantage of feeding in terminally ill patients. It may therefore be better to choose an individual who is emotionally removed from the situation and can implement your living will to the letter. It is also important to choose someone who resides in the same city as you do, and it may be better to choose someone who does not stand to gain or lose anything from your staying alive or passing on...at least not knowingly. The agent must be at least eighteen years old— some states require the agent to be twenty-one—and there are certain exclusions. For instance, the agent should not be your health-care provider or the owner or operator of a health-care or residential-care facility that services you. The agent may also not be an employee or the spouse or an employee of your health-care provider. You can change your mind about your agent at any time by destroying the document or writing *revoked* on it and signing each page.

The second wish is the kind of medical treatment you will accept or refuse. For instance, you may decide that you do not want to be on a ventilator even if it means an end to your life. You might also decide that you do not want to be in pain and that everything possible should be done to ensure you are pain free, even if this means you end up permanently in a drug-induced coma in order not to feel pain, a term referred to as *palliative sedation* in palliative medicine. I recently had a patient under my care in an inpatient hospice setting; she was in her early thirties and had bilateral breast cancer that had spread widely. She was in a lot of pain and really wanted to end it all. Euthanasia—mercy killing—is a crime. Physician-assisted suicide, on the other hand, is endorsed only by a few states and should not be confused with euthanasia. The state I practice in does not endorse either. It took me almost a day to explain the difference to this patient and her family members. Eventually she was palliatively sedated to the appreciation of her family, and she passed on peacefully a couple of weeks later, pain free. You may state that you do not want certain treatment if all it serves is to prolong life without any quality.

The third wish is the degree of comfort you want. This has to do with pain, fever, dehydration, music, and personal grooming like shaving or clipping of nails.

The fourth wish has to do with how you want to be treated by others. For instance, you might want members of your church or religious organization to pray around you. You might want to have people around you or no one around you or to be kept clean at all times.

The last wish is what you want your loved ones to know about you and what you want them to tell others about you. The form will then have to be signed and witnessed by preferably two individuals, and then copies are made and deposited with your physician, family members, and your attorney if you wish.

End of Life

This is as certain as taxes and being born. Everyone would like to die "peacefully in their sleep" but not everyone will have this privilege. Some of my patients with chronic illness rationalize their noncompliance with and nonadherence to medical treatment to the fact that everyone has to die of something. This, in my opinion, is a nonissue; the issue is the amount of disability and suffering one undergoes before dying.

I remember visiting a patient of mine in the hospital during rounds one morning. He had been noncompliant with my constant advice and had just suffered a massive stroke; his speech was garbled but you could still make out his words. However, he could not move a half of his body, and was being bathed and cleaned by a nurse's aide after a bowel movement. I asked him if he was hurting, and he said, "Only my pride, Doc, only my pride. I wish I had listened to you." He later told me that death was a far better option than living like that. I'm sure if he had a way to end his life he would not hesitate to do it.

Some people prefer to die at home; others prefer to die in a facility like a hospice where they are guaranteed a certain amount of dignity and comfort. A lot of people are petrified by the term *hospice*. Patients qualify for hospice care when two physicians certify that if the disease runs its normal course they have a life expectancy of six months or less. No one knows when anyone will die, just like we do not know exactly when people will be born—apart from women who have an elective Cesarean section. Working in a hospice I can tell you that the same principles of working in a hospital hold true. We can never predict exactly when a patient will pass on. A lot of family members ask us, "How much longer?" The truth is no one knows exactly when a patient will take his or her last breath. We can predict in some cases to minutes or hours, but some clients can show several signs of impending death and still linger for several hours to a few days. I have left the hospice several times at night only to be called later and told about the transition of certain patients that I least expected would pass on that night. This always humbles me and proves to me time and time again that there are greater forces than we understand.

In certain situations we can predict how much longer people have to live. For instance, individuals who are on dialysis generally live for about seven to ten days after stopping the dialysis. One thing I have learned in the hospice world, however, is that a lot of the clients hold on for something, somebody, or an event. Sometimes they just wait for family members to let go and say it is okay. Others want to exit as soon as no one is looking or as soon as the family goes for a cup of coffee or a meal. Clients who can speak always talk about going "home," and they are usually very precise about when they are going. Some have a large bowel movement or are terminally agitated or have a surge of energy and have a conversation with the family and eat beyond everyone's expectation—what we call the last rally.

An issue that comes up every now and then is that of feeding. Despite living wills that state the contrary, a lot of family members are uncomfortable about not feeding their loved ones as their life draws to an end. Some studies have been published that conclude that feeding does not improve the comfort level of the dying patient. Some people say when the clients are semiconscious they lose the sensation of hunger, and therefore feeding them does not provide any benefit and may, in fact, hasten their death. Some family members want everything possible to be done to feed elderly demented relatives. Some of them are aspirating, and once that occurs in a demented patient it usually signifies the beginning of the end regardless of the intervention that is carried out.

Medical Bills

I think it is appropriate to discuss hospital bills at this point. You will receive a bill from every consultant who sees you in the hospital, or rather every specialty that sees you, whether the physicians are on your insurance plan or not. Hospital charges are totally different from physician charges. These are also different from pathology charges, and yes, no one asks you if it is okay; they just bill you. For instance, say you undergo a colonoscopy and the doctor resects a couple of polyps. In order to ascertain the nature of the polyp so as to recommend further care, the specimen is sent to a pathologist, but you probably won't know it until the bill arrives! All the gastroenterologist will tell you is that he or she took some polyps out and will let you know if they are malignant or not. You are probably thinking the gastroen-terologist will look at the polyps and let you know. Wrong! They send it to a pathologist, and worse still, the pathologist may not accept your insurance and therefore charges you the full price because you are out of network! How about the consultant that is asked to see you in the hospital? He or she may be out of network as well. Some consultants are

116

very good about this, however, and will inform you that you are out of network to them and you will need to be seen by someone else. This is only if it is not an emergency; in urgent cases we save lives first and ask about the ability to pay later.

Some hospital emergency rooms have started a policy of demanding co-pays from people who visit the emergency room and are deemed not to have a real emergency. I have talked to some emergency room administrators as to the rationale behind this, and they say the number one reason is to try and discourage people from crowding emergency rooms with none emergencies so the staff can concentrate on real emergencies. The second is to ensure better collections from the emergency room billing. A lot of bills from the emergency room have to be sent to a collections agency. A lot of people have co-pays and deductibles that were hitherto not being collected by the billing department in the emergency rooms. One of the reasons why it takes so long to be seen in a doctor's office as well as in an emergency room is the insurance verification process. We have come a long way from the days this process was done by phone and fax. Nowadays insurance verification for most insurance companies is done electronically, speeding up the process a great deal.

Co-pay is the amount that must be paid at the time of service, and this amount varies depending on the place of service. For instance, a doctor's office may have a co-pay of twenty dollars while the emergency room may have a co-pay of one hundred dollars and an urgent care center fifty dollars. Some insurance companies are beginning to penalize their members for visiting the emergency room. The co-pay for an emergency room visits for a non-emergent condition that does not result in an admission is higher than what you will pay if you are indeed admitted.

Once you are admitted the meter starts to run. You are charged for *everything*, and I mean it—from the disposables that are used in your care to the medications you use and the food you eat and the investigations you demand or need. I take care of a very meticulous elderly couple; his wife accompanies him to every physician appointment and writes everything down. A lot of physicians are uncomfortable with this, but it is only so she can remember what transpires during the encounter for future reference. Anyway, anytime either the husband or the wife is admitted to the hospital they go with all their medications and insist that they take their home medicines and are not supplied their home medications by the hospital. She explained to me once that when she saw the bill from the hospital for certain medications during one of her husband's admissions she swore she would always take her home medications with her to the hospital and ask the physician for permission to take them while in hospital. No one has said no yet!

So you are billed for the food you eat, every X-ray, ultrasound, and physician you see. The radiological investigations results in at least two bills, one for the procedure and the other for the interpretation by the radiologist. Some of them may be "out of your network" but will still see you and send you a bill that your insurance company cannot negotiate. You see, as physicians we all agree to a discounted fee for more business. What I mean by this is that my fees for seeing a new patient with a complex problem may be $250 dollars, but I may agree to see patients from an insurance company for $150 resulting in a discount of $100 because they will send me a lot of patients, so this is a sort of "wholesale" price. I am also forbidden from billing the member for the balance. However, anyone who walks off the street will be charged the full price of $250 because that is the "retail" price. The tricky part of this is that I cannot just give a discount unless I document hardship. I can see the patient for free, but I cannot arbitrarily bill him or her something far less, as this can be deemed to be discriminatory and is a way to avoid discrimination in the fee structure. For instance, if someone comes in whom I perceive to be wealthy, what stops me from charging $400? On the other hand, someone who is really poor can be charged $50; this is discriminatory, as everyone should be charged the same amount.

Anywhere from two weeks to three months after discharge, the bills start to pour in. Some of them you will recognize and some you will not. For instance, if you are expecting a bill from me, you will not see my name on the bill but the name of the practice. The first thing that shows up, if you have insurance, is the explanation of benefits, also called the EOB for short. This explains whom the bill is from and in some cases the business name of the practice, and what the procedure was. This is usually in a number code called the evaluation and management code. It may include , your providers name and cost of the procedure carried out on you, e.g., a CT scan of the abdomen and the pelvis. The reason for this EOB is so the insurance company can alert you that someone claiming to be you has benefited from the services listed, and if that person is not you they expect to hear from you as soon as possible. So if you agree the EOB is a true representation of what services you benefited from, the insurance company now tells you ahead of the hospital and physician bills how much they will cover and how much you have to pay. This gives you a heads up, and you can decide to call the hospital or the physician's office to work out a payment plan for your portion. Ignoring the EOB and then the bill is the beginning of credit problems. The hospital and physician's office will send you to collections. Sometimes for people with no insurance the hospital writes off the bill or approves the patient for indigent care after a long and drawn-out process. The hospital and the physician are different entities, however, so just because one has accepted you as a charity case does not mean the other will. As a self-pay you can always negotiate the bills you get; physician's offices are always the easiest to deal with. After agreeing on a discount you might want to get this in writing and also settle it quickly so that in case the physician sells the practice, your name will not be forwarded to a collections agency as one of the practice's debtors. As a self-pay you can negotiate with everyone who sends you a bill. There is no rule of any ratios because in most cases when we see an individual is uninsured we know the chances of collecting anything from that person are almost zero; therefore whatever we are able to collect is a plus.

In some cases the insurance company classifies the illness as a preexisting condition and therefore does not pay the bill. I remember one of the patients I admitted through the emergency room some time ago. He had gallstone pancreatitis, which turned really bad, and he almost lost his life. Prior to being admitted he was just starting a new life with a new wife and had just bought a car repair shop business, which he was eager to start running. After spending less than a week in the hospital his insurance company denied his hospitalization saying his illness had a preexisting condition—gallstones! I was livid on behalf of this man, and you can imagine how he felt when he finally recovered. He had lost his garage and his new relationship had hit the rocks, and he was extremely grateful for the care he got but was unable to pay. He swore he was going to report the insurance company to the state insurance commissioner and promised I would be paid my physician fees no matter how long it took. It has been over five years now and I still have not heard from him. I hope he is still doing well, and I wonder how his battle with the insurance company is going.

Office bills are easier to handle than hospital ones. One of the main issues is the labs that are used in offices and if they are in network or not. The other issue is that a lot of physicians now carry out diagnostic testing in their offices, so ensure that they are covered by your insurance company before a test is carried out and if not try to negotiate with your physician *before* the test is done. At least ask and let someone check it out for you, or better still have something in writing stating that the tests are fully covered by your insurance company especially if it is a very expensive test.

Do not wait until you have a serious health condition before you have a health-care strategy for you and your family. Seek out free clinics or clinics that will see you for a discounted price, especially if you have a chronic health condition like hypertension or diabetes. You can always negotiate with clinics and, of course, ask for the generic medications that are much cheaper than brand names.

There are grants available to women for free mammograms depending on where they live. An Internet search should reveal those in existence in your part of the country. Alternatively, you can always call your local hospital radiology department to find out if there are grants available for mammograms. I have assisted several of my patients in getting free mammograms with our local hospitals.

Not having health insurance is not the end of the world; you can still care for yourself reasonably well even without it. If you are poor you may qualify for Medicaid through the Department of Family and Children's Services. If you are above age sixty-two or disabled, you may qualify for Medicare. Check with your local Social Security office and you will be guided as to the process of getting help. In some cases you qualify for both Medicare and Medicaid all depending on your particular circumstances. Also, understand your insurance policy as well as the deductibles and premiums. Understand how much your deductible is and if you will be able to achieve it. There is also a co-pay that is due at the time of service; this can range from two dollars for state-sponsored Medicaid to thirty-five dollars or more for some PPO plans. At this point I must point out that *all* co-pays are due at the time of service, and physicians are mandated by the insurance company to collect all co-pays. Failure to do so can be regarded as a form of enticement to the patient from the physician.

Understand the health savings account, which is becoming more and more popular. Do not believe all that the salesman tells you; do your own research so you understand *all* aspects of your policy. Should you face a situation where your employer is changing insurance carriers but you like your doctors and do not want to change them, ensure that you ask your physicians if they accept the new insurance company you have in mind before you sign on the dotted line. In general, the preferred provider organizations (PPO) are the best policies to have. They are also the most expensive and cover the most medications. The Health Maintenance Organizations are generally speaking the most restrictive; however, some insurance is much better than none, and if an HMO is all you can afford, so be it. I would actually prefer a HMO with its own clinics and hospitals like Kaiser Permanente, which also employs a large number of specialists, and referrals within the system are virtually seamless. Other forms of insurance include the government-run ones, which include Medicaid, Medicare, and the Veterans Administration System that defines individuals as partially or fully service connected. Generally speaking, the state-sponsored Medicaid program caters to the indigent as well as those who are considered earning below the poverty level. The guidelines vary from state to state, and in a lot of states Medicaid clients are encouraged to join one HMO or the other as a way of controlling cost. At one time in the state of Georgia, Medicaid was one of the best kinds of insurance to have from the point of view of the consumer. This is because it used to cover almost all medications as well as investigations with the minimum cost or hassle. A lot of physicians did not accept it then because of very low reimbursement rates, as well as the amount of hassle involved in caring for the patients. The situation is even worse now because of the HMO system. These companies, in my opinion, are even more restrictive than the traditional Medicaid services. They also have a very short list of accepting specialists, thereby making it extremely difficult for primary care providers to refer patients to specialists. Fewer and fewer specialists are accepting Medicaid and even less so the Medicaid HMOS.

In my opinion if your employer provides health insurance go for the PPO first if you can afford it. Second best are the HMO plans and also explore the possibility of government or state sponsored plans. If all fails seek the health department, free clinics, or medical schools for your health care needs. The internet is a very useful tool for this so engage a relative who is very internet savvy to research this for you if you do not have the know-how but never give up.

CHAPTER 6

Immunization and Screening

As an internist as well as a designated United States Civil Surgeon by the United States Citizenship and Immigration Services, I am frequently confronted with issues of adult shots. According to the American Medical Association, about fifty thousand adults and adolescents in the United States die from preventable diseases. The public needs to be informed of these immunizations so they can demand them from their physicians in order to be afforded protection.

There is a series of shots recommended for adults. The most common are the human papillomavirus (HPV) shots for young females and males, the flu shot, the pneumococcal shot, and the herpes zoster (shingles) shot. I recall one of my most precious adult patients who asked me about the herpes shingles shot several years ago even though she had previously suffered from chicken pox. Needless to say I did not encourage her to get the shot, and you would be right if you guessed that she did get shingles—and she also suffered from the extremely painful complication of the rash called post-herpetic neuralgia, which is a nerve pain complication of shingles. I was able to provide her immediate relief with samples of a medication that is approved for this kind of pain, and she got better quickly. When she found out how expensive the medications I was giving her for free were, she was easily able to forget the fact that I did not encourage her to take the vaccine.

All adults above sixty regardless of a previous history of chicken pox are recommended to get the shingles immunization if they have not had the vaccine before in the past. It is estimated that only two percent of the population over sixty receive the vaccine, and we therefore have a long way to go. Please, if you are reading this and you have any relatives that are over sixty, encourage them by any means necessary to get the shingles shot. This condition as well as the complications after can be very painful, but it is preventable. Some people cannot take certain vaccinations, and your doctor will guide you if you fall into any one of the groups of people who cannot take this vaccine. The most common reaction to this vaccine and most vaccines in general are in the form of local reactions like redness, pain, swelling, and itching. Any vaccine, like any medication, can cause a hypersensitivity reaction or an allergic reaction, which can occur a few minutes to a few hours after receiving the vaccine.

The annual flu shot used to be recommended only for adults fifty years and over, but recently the group has been expanded to include the eighteen to fifty age group. There are two types of the vaccine, the live attenuated (weakened) one as well as the inactivated one. The live attenuated one is the intranasal one and has more contraindications than the inactivated one. If you are in doubt, always consult your physician before taking the shots in non-physician or -pharmacist supervised settings. A previous allergy to an immunization may be the grounds for withholding any future immunization of the same kind. Children younger than nine years old who are receiving the vaccine for the first time or who missed the second dose the year before will need two doses of the vaccine separated by at least four weeks for both types of the vaccine. Patients must realize that influenza is a serious respiratory illness caused by a virus. According to the American Medical Association it causes an average of thirty-six thousand deaths yearly and over two hundred thousand hospitalizations. The vaccination is usually about 70–90 percent effective in preventing influenza in healthy adults and children. Even if the strain of virus that infects a previously immunized person is different from the strain immunized against, the illness will be less severe.

The pneumococcal polysaccharide shot is also recommended for adults over the age of sixty-five or anybody with chronic medical conditions like heart disease, liver disease, kidney problems, alcoholism, diabetes, people who smoke, people who have leakage of cerebrospinal fluid—fluid around the brain—or people who are electively going to have their spleen removed for a variety of reasons, as well as people who reside in nursing homes, assisted living, and any such similar settings. The vaccine can be given as a single dose or in the form of two doses. It protects against infections that the elderly are vulnerable to as well as bugs that can cause other serious infections of the blood, brain, or spinal cord. The infection can be fatal sometimes and is passed from individual to individual by coughing sneezing or any way that aerosolizes body fluids. Because the vaccine is commonly referred to as the pneumonia shot (against the AMA's recommendation) patients often erroneously feel it protects them against all types of pneumonia for life.

Hepatitis shots can be for hepatitis A or B. The shots come in a combined formula and can also be given individually. This is one of those vaccines that is recommended for everyone in the health-care field or people who come in contact with body fluids regularly, as well as those who have household or sexual contact with people with chronic hepatitis; and also dialysis patients, alcoholics, people who are traveling to an endemic area, or men who have sex with men or drug users. Depending on the situation you may qualify for one vaccine or the other or both. There are ways you can check if you are immune to the virus by blood tests, but it might be cheaper to go ahead and receive the vaccines instead of checking for the immunity. The hepatitis B virus is usually given in three doses while the hepatitis A is given in two doses; however, this sometimes depends on the make and the brands in question. Once you start the series, ensure you complete it because an incomplete series will not confer complete protection. If you move or change doctors it is your responsibility to inform your new health-care provider what you need and when you need it. In case you cannot get to a physician on time for the next shot, you can always call the closest health department to find out how to complete your series. Failure to complete the series in a timely manner may result in having to start the whole series all over again.

Hepatitis A is spread by close contact and often by eating contaminated food or drinking contaminated water. A person with the virus can easily pass it on to other members of the same household. According to the CDC in the year 2004 more than twenty thousand people were infected with Hepatitis A, and about fifty died from the disease. The symptoms may include flu-like illness with abdominal pains and diarrhea, and some patients may develop a yellow discoloration of the eyes. About 20 percent of people with the disease will have to be hospitalized. Hepatitis B is also a virus that affects the liver; according to the CDC about fifty thousand people become infected with the virus on a yearly basis. About a million people are chronically infected, and thousands die from the complications of the illness. These complications include cirrhosis as well as liver cancer. The infection can be spread by infected blood and bodily fluids; even sharing toothbrushes with an infected person can lead to the infection. Newborns can be infected at birth if their mothers are infected. People with Hepatitis B can be totally asymptomatic until late stages of the disease.

Tetanus, diphtheria, and pertussis shots are recommended for adults who do not have written documentation of a completed series beforehand, or for adults who have a wound and whose last tetanus shot is over five years old. It is recommended that adults get a booster of the tetanus and diphtheria vaccine—Td—every ten years. Using the tetanus toxoid alone in people without a previous history of immunization is not recommended. Tetanus is an infection that that can cause muscle spasms and tightening of muscles called "lockjaw." Diphtheria is an upper respiratory infection that can cause a thick membrane to form in the back of the throat. It can cause paralysis, heart failure, and even death in some cases. The pertussis is also known as whooping cough, which causes coughing spells and vomiting. It is known in some circles as the ninety-day cough. The CDC states that it has recently seen increased resurgence in the cases of whooping cough in the US.

The polio vaccine is recommended for immigrants who have no proof of previous immunization and also for residents of the United States who plan to travel to polio-endemic areas of the world, like my country of birth, Nigeria. It can cause paralysis as well as death. The virus gains entrance into the body through the mouth. Even though the last case of polio in the US was in 1979, it still occurs in some parts of the world; so in order to reduce the risk of importation to the US from other countries the vaccination must be continued. There are two types of vaccines available: the oral polio vaccine, which is the less common, and the inactivated polio vaccine, which is used more commonly in the United States.

The chicken pox vaccine, also known as varicella, is recommended for people without evidence of immunity. This is usually given in two doses. Chicken pox is a highly contagious disease and is spread by coughing or sneezing or by contact with fluid from the chicken pox blisters. The infection can end up in the brain or the lungs. When it infects a pregnant woman, it can cause birth defects and even fetal death. Most people who get this vaccine will not develop chicken pox, and even if they do it will be a very mild form. However, someone who has had chicken pox in the past can still develop shingles years later. People with evidence of immunity include those with a history of chicken pox or shingles, and complications of the infection occur more in adults than in children.

The meningococcal vaccine is recommended for young adults and college freshmen. You have probably heard of this outbreak in colleges or dormitories. The vaccine is also recommended to individuals who are traveling to endemic areas like the so-called "meningitis belt" of sub-Saharan Africa, or to people who do not have a functional spleen and whose spleen has been removed. The bacteria can cause meningitis, a fatal infection of the covering of the brain as well as the spinal cord that can lead to death in about ten percent of the people it infects.

The measles, mumps, and rubella vaccine is recommended for people born after 1957, who should receive at least one dose if they have not been immunized previously. Measles is a virus infection caused by coughing or sneezing. Mumps is also a virus infection that can lead to fever, headaches, and swollen glands. Rubella is also known as German measles, and if it infects a pregnant woman she may miscarry or the baby may be born with birth defects.

High-risk personnel like health-care workers and international travelers are also recommended to receive a total of two doses.

The newest kid on the block regarding immunizations is the human papillomavirus vaccine, which is recommended for women less than twenty-six years of age to prevent cervical cancer and genital warts. One brand is also approved for boys and men age nine to twenty-six to prevent genital warts. Preferably it is given prior to becoming sexually active. There are two types of the vaccines currently on the market. These vaccines do not protect against all types of HPV or treat HPV if you are already infected. It is to be avoided during pregnancy and is given in three doses; the cost and inconsistent insurance coverage currently limits its use.

In the United states HPV is the most common sexually transmitted disease, and there are over one hundred strains of the virus. Most of the time the infection with the virus does not cause any symptoms, but some infections can lead to cervical cancer, which is the second leading cause of cancer deaths among women worldwide. It can also cause genital warts. The vaccine targets 70 percent of cervical cancers and about 90 percent of genital warts. Even after getting the vaccine, girls and women will still need to be screened for cervical cancer every three years because not all cancer-causing strains are included in the vaccine. According to some sources, about half of all men and women are infected with the virus at some point in their lives.

The above is obviously an oversimplification of the adult immunization schedule. The message to take away from this is for you to determine which shots you think you can benefit from and to discuss this with your doctor.

There is a great deal of suspicion of the general public regarding immunizations as well as a lot of misconceptions. I have had patients tell me time and time again that they do not take shots because it makes them fall sick. My answer to this is to ask if an immunization preceded them falling ill every single time they have been ill in the past. The answer is always no. I then use my most favorite analogy that the fact that the dog crossed the road just before the cat died does not mean the dog is responsible for the death of the cat. There are usually several factors that contribute to a disease process, and concluding that the effect of an immunization is always an illness is unscientific. I do, however, agree that not all shots are for everyone, and that is why everyone should be screened thoroughly to see if they will benefit from certain shots. I understand the public's anxiety over new shots like the H1N1 immunization. I could not even get my wife to agree to immunize our kids against the H1N1 virus. I rest my case!

Whenever you plan to travel, please visit the CDC Web site at least four to six weeks before you plan to depart in order to research your destination and be informed on the vaccines needed before you travel.

Health Maintenance

Here is a quick rundown of the generally accepted screening tests for adults ages nineteen to sixty-four.

- Height and weight and assessment of Body Mass Index.
- Blood pressure screening at each health-care encounter. I would personally encourage each individual to monitor blood pressure at home on a regular basis.
- Vision/glaucoma screening every three years for African-Americans between the ages of twenty and thirty-nine or anyone with a family history of glaucoma; every two to four years regardless of race between the ages of forty and fifty-four; and every one to three years between the ages of fifty-five and sixty-four.
- Hearing assessment and prompt referral if there are any concerns.
- Fasting lipid profile at five-year intervals if no problems exist. This includes total, HDL, LDL, and triglycerides.
- Tuberculin skin tests for individuals at a high risk.
- Diabetes screening every three years after the age of forty-five for individuals at a high risk and others with high cholesterol and hypertension.
- Bone density screening for osteoporosis for women older than sixty at increased risk and also on chronic steroid use.
- Depression screening of individuals based on behavior and emotions.
- Cognitive screening based on changes in performance with age.

- Sexually transmitted disease screening to include HIV, Chlamydia—for sexually active females above twenty-five— gonorrhea, and syphilis screening.

Cancer Screening in Males

- Testicular cancer screening at physician's discretion.
- Prostate cancer screening depending on family history and race.
- Colonoscopy every ten years beginning at age fifty. Further schedule will depend on the findings of first test. Sigmoidoscopy every five years or annual fecal occult blood testing are alternatives.
- Abdominal aortic screening by ultrasound for men age sixty-five to seventy-five with a history of smoking.

Cancer Screening in Females

- Clinical breast examination by a physician annually.
- Monthly breast examination by patient after proper instruction by physician.
- Mammography every one to two years for ages forty and older.
- Cervical cancer screening within three years of becoming sexually active or by age twenty-one, whichever is sooner. Thereafter annual pap test up to age thirty. For women thirty and over, after three negative results screening can be reduced to every two to three years. If pap and HPV are negative, screening can be done every three years. Pap smears can be stopped in

females above sixty-five if they have had no abnormal results over the past ten years.

- Colonoscopy every ten years beginning at age fifty. Further schedule will depend on the findings of first test. Sigmoidoscopy every five years or annual fecal occult blood testing are alternatives.

Over age sixty-five there should more emphasis on immunizations including the following:

- Tetanus and diphtheria vaccines.
- Influenza vaccines.
- Hepatitis A and B vaccines.
- Measles, mumps, and rubella, one dose for adults born after 1956 without evidence of immunity.
- Shingles administered one time for adults over age sixty.
- Chicken pox for all adults without evidence of immunity. Administer two shots four to eight weeks apart.

If you or your loved one has a special situation and are unsure about the frequency of screening, you may contact your physician for clarification. Please ensure you have information on all previous screenings as well as what the outcome was before asking for your doctor's opinion.

CHAPTER 7

Infections

This book would not be complete without a brief discussion of infections. A lot of patients believe that antibiotics will cure any type of infection. Well, I have news for you: there are different kinds organisms that cause infections. The broad categories are bacteria, viruses, and fungi, and one size doesn't fit all when it comes to curing one or the other. (There are other categories that are beyond the scope of this book.) So we use antibiotics for bacterial infections, antivirals for viral infections, and antifungals for fungal infections. In each of these categories there are hundreds of families with hundreds of subsets, and each family member is a unique bug; the fact that a member of that particular bug family is killed by a certain medication does not mean the same medication will affect all the other members of the family.

Let me walk you through the process of treating an infection. Let's say an individual—Grandma—has a urinary tract infection. We identify this by her symptoms, a physical examination, and by microscopic examination of the urine. In medical school microbiology we are taught about the bugs that commonly cause a urinary tract infection. The lab in most hospitals releases an antibiogram for the most common bugs causing urinary tract infections in Grandma's geographic area. We decide on an antibiotic based on the knowledge of these bugs and what medication they are sensitive to. Finally we look at her adverse reactions and allergy profile before deciding which medication is the best. So we put Grandma on the medication, and you expect her to get better immediately! But it doesn't happen that way; initially the antibiotic will have to get into her system to start working. Depending on the antibiotic, it may take three to five days to begin working after taking it by mouth. Shots, of course, work faster.

Usually urinary infections are caused by bacteria, but what if in the case of Grandma it is actually a fungus causing the infection? Will the antibiotic work? Of course not! The urine will have to be sent to the lab to grow in a culture medium in order to identify the bug. This process can take anywhere from one day to six weeks! What happens to Grandma during this period? Depending on how sick she is we can put her on both an antifungal and an antibacterial initially, only to narrow it down once the bug has been identified. After identifying the bug, the lab carries out more tests, called *sensitivity* tests, in a petri dish in the laboratory to determine what medication will actually kill the bug. In some cases the bug is killed in the petri dish in a laboratory but then when you use the same medication in the individual it does not work for various reasons.

So I will recap. When you have an infection it could be bacterial, viral, or fungal, generally speaking. You are put on a medication based on your physician's knowledge of the common bugs that cause the same type of infection in that community. Meanwhile samples of the fluid from the affected area are sent to the lab. After three days pass and there is no improvement, there are many possibilities, some of which are listed below:

- The initial choice of antibiotics is not effective against the bug.
- The initial site of assumed infection is wrong.
- It may not be bacteria causing the infection.
- The bug is resistant to the antibiotic.
- The patient is not taking the medication as prescribed.
- The bug identified in the urine is not causing any problems.

Sometimes you hear your doctor saying he or she is going to ask an infectious diseases expert to see you. These are doctors who specialize in using anti-infectives to treat people. In the US these are the individuals who also treat patients with HIV, though in some countries hematologists treat HIV infected patients. I have taken the time to explain this process in detail because individuals and their relatives believe results of cultures of body fluids are available immediately! Tuberculosis cultures can take as long as six weeks to be resulted. So can some viral and fungal cultures.

In some viral and bacterial infections, some indirect means of identification are used. The most common is the nasal swab we use to identify the flu virus that takes a few minutes. We also have a rapid strep screen that can detect a strep throat in minutes. Please note that these tests also have their limitations. When they are negative, it does not mean that the individual does not have the disease; and when positive it also does not confirm the disease. The physician has to decide whether or not to treat. Complicated? Welcome to the physician's world. Your physician will explain to you exactly what he or she is doing and why. This information gives you the baseline to understand what you are being told and the process involved, so you can ask meaningful questions.

There are two things that can happen in general when an infection is not treated. It may burn itself out—very common in viral illnesses—or cause a prolonged illness and sometimes death. This brings me to the case of an unfortunate gentleman I admitted several months ago. This man presented to the emergency room delirious with a very low blood pressure and was unable to tell us anything. He obviously had a severe infection taking place, but we could not locate a source. We tried to get a urine sample but found that we could not pass a catheter through his urinary meatus. We talked to his wife, who said that after a motor vehicle accident a few years ago her husband had been unable to urinate normally. He used a rusty hanger to pass a catheter through his umbilical area to his bladder to drain urine! He did this for years and his wife never raised an objection. By the time he arrived in the ER that night his abdominal cavity was filled with pus. He died that night. The lesson here is that you should never be passive when you see your loved one doing something to his or her body that your common sense tells you is wrong. I suggest you immediately accompany your loved one to a visit with his or her physician and then ask the physician in your loved one's presence about the risky behavior.

An organism that a lot of people are aware of and are scared of these days is the methicillin resistant staphylococcus aureus, commonly referred to as MRSA. Staph are bacteria that commonly live on the skin as well as the nostrils. They can become disease-causing bacteria once there is a breach in the continuity of the skin. A lot of people refer to this breach as "spider bites." These bacteria have become resistant to a lot of antibiotics, just like some others are beginning to be as well. We are all responsible for this due to the widespread use of antibiotics for minor and even viral illnesses resulting in the evolution of some resistant bugs, which continue to be a challenge to the medical community, especially in nursing homes. Anyone can be infected with MRSA, and the infection may be mild or serious and life threatening. If one person in the family gets it, the infection may spread to other members of the family. It may affect any part of the body. Contrary to what a lot of people think you cannot diagnose MRSA by merely looking at a boil, a physician can suspect MRSA but the confirmation comes from a laboratory after sending specimens. You can have an active infection or be a carrier. Carriers do not have any active disease but can pass it on to other people. Remember Typhoid Mary? If you have the bug, be especially careful around people with a weak immune system like newborn babies and the elderly or people with chronic diseases like diabetes. You must exercise universal precautions with your sores and any fluids coming from where your infection is. MRSA can be treated; you must follow your doctor's advice and take your medications as prescribed, and more importantly complete the course prescribed to you. Sometimes the infection needs to be treated by intravenous antibiotics for a certain duration of time. Do not stop taking your medications when you feel better, and if you have any questions ask your health-care provider or your local health department.

APPENDIX

Guidance in Choosing a Nursing Home
Genie Trafford, RN-BC, RAC-CT

One of the most difficult decisions you could probably make involves placing a loved one in a nursing home. While many facilities are called "rehab centers," "nursing centers," "skilled nursing facilities," or "health and rehab," they are all synonymous with the phrase "nursing home." Any way you look at it, these facilities are designed to care for our most precious and often forgotten generation, the elderly. Nursing homes many years ago focused primarily on the aged population. In the 1900s many impoverished citizens went to "almshouses." There, the unfortunate lived in crumbling buildings and received substandard care, if any care at all.

By the late 1960s legislation was in place to raise the standards of facilities and improve the care provided in the nursing home. Following reports on the nursing home industry by the Institute of Medicine in 1985, one of the largest overhauls of federal regulations was contained in the Omnibus Reconciliation Act (OBRA) in 1987. Many changes and challenges have taken place since then in order to provide the best quality care for the aged. The nursing home industry has grown to help the many needs of the elderly. But with the boom in the geriatric population, are facilities ready for the increased need? Approximately 12 percent of the population is over sixty-five, and this number is expected to increase to 20 percent by 2030. Approximately 1.7 million people live in one of the seventeen thousand nursing facilities across the United States. As you can see, the nursing home industry plays a vital role in the continuum of care from hospitals or communities to settings where the elders can receive needed medical care.

Today, many facilities care for patients/residents of all ages. Regardless of the age of the patient, the facility's primary goal is to provide the highest practicable level of function for the duration of the person's stay. Within these pages, I hope to share with you the basics of nursing home settings, payment options, support services, and other available resources to help you in your decision making. I will also share some of my personal experiences in the nursing home setting.

One evening while Nurse M was working, Ms. J (an eighty-year-old resident) came streaking down the hall in her underwear, yelling out, "Super sex!" As she passed by Mr. W's room, he looked out and yelled back, "I'll just have the soup."

At the age of six, I remember telling my grandmother that I wanted to be a nurse. I really never wavered in my dream to put Band-Aids on more than just my teddy bears. In high school, I decided to try my hand at working in the local nursing home in town. My mom had said that would be a "surefire" way to find out if I liked taking care of people. So, I was hired one day and went to work the very next day...no special skills required. I was called an "aide" back then and was making $3.20 an hour.

Today, there are specific training programs for those who want to be "aides," and they must meet the training requirements and pass the tests of a state-approved course. They are now referred to as CNAs (certified nursing assistants) or PCTs (personal care techs), and the pay is certainly a lot more. Of course, for the work they do, they are worth their weight in gold!

When I was hired I went to work with Annie, one of the senior aides on staff. In those days, we didn't worry about blood-borne illnesses (AIDS, hepatitis, etc.) or the H1N1 flu outbreaks. We just focused on making sure our patients were clean, dry, dressed appropriately, and out of bed for one of the 3Bs activities (bowling, Bible, or BINGO). It didn't take long for me to get hooked! From the sweet, gray-haired lady who loved to grab my hand with her sticky one and tell me she loved me, to the little elderly gentleman, who quickly and quietly would try to pinch me as I passed by, each one, with all their precious stories of the good old days, kept me coming back for more.

I continued working as an aide while in nursing school, and when I became an RN in 1989, I returned to that same facility. I had the opportunity to serve as the nurse aide instructor and teach men and women one of the most rewarding jobs of all, caring for another human being. I transitioned within the company to yet another position, the Director of Nursing (DON). While I transferred to another building, I never forgot the staff or patients who inspired me to keep going. Serving as a DON was yet another eye-opening experience! I was in charge of ensuring quality care to 182 patients and managing nearly that many staff! From dealing with family members who needed to vent, those who had valid concerns, staff who had their own personal matters, and doctors and pharmacists trying to ensure everything was done correctly, to the all-time-consuming budget, I was able to serve in the same facility as their DON for ten years—and wouldn't change one minute of it!

Throughout my years in the nursing home setting, I was trained in the newest rules and regulations regarding the industry. I learned the newest tools used for assessing patients and collecting data with focused outcomes on better quality of care. All of this helped to prepare me for my current position in an eighty-nine-bed skilled nursing facility where I serve as the Medicare assessment coordinator. In my twenty years of geriatric nursing, this has been by far my favorite job and where I want to remain in my career. I am able to see patients needing rehab come in with conditions that have affected their overall mobility and health, who then overcome these obstacles, most of them returning to the community. But how do they get there in the first place? Who pays for it? What's the first step? OK, here's where you want to start taking notes!

Guidance in Choosing a Nursing Home

Most often, the decision to transition to a nursing home is made due to a medical condition. Many people only think about the hospital setting or independent living and often overlook the supportive services from a nursing home to improve and maintain health. Whether patients are there for just a few weeks of therapy or for the remainder of their years, the nursing home setting can provide piece of mind to loved ones and quality care and comfort to the patient. Most facilities refer to their patients as *residents* or *clients*. Our facility refers to them as residents, and that will be how they are addressed here.

Most often residents are considered for nursing home admission while they are still in the hospital setting being treated for an acute medical condition (fractured hip, stroke, knee replacement, etc.). Depending upon the support services available to the residents and family, it will be determined if the nursing home setting can assist in helping residents regain their independence and return to the community. Sometimes it is obvious that a resident will need permanent placement in the nursing home.

Admitting a loved one to a nursing home brings about many feelings of anxiety, grief, guilt, and depression. The staff in the nursing home setting is very helpful to the family and resident in working through these quite normal emotions. Residents who reside permanently make friends, become like family to the staff, participate in the many activities and functions within the facility, and are overall satisfied with the care and services they receive. Some residents, however, never adjust to permanent placement and get pulled into depression, grieving, and even acting out in front of the family or playing favorites. Staff pulls out all the stops to help these people adjust, but sometimes they can literally grieve themselves to death.

Nursing homes can be hospital based, managed by big corporations, or owned by a local family; and can be for profit or not for profit. My administrator used to say, "We're a not-for-profit facility, but we're also a not-for-loss facility." The nursing home industry is a business, and there are budgets to be managed, expenses to control, supplies to buy, and rules with which to comply. Many facilities accept payment from Medicare and Medicaid and Veterans Administration Benefits. These facilities enter into a contract with the government agencies and must maintain compliance with regulations in order to continue to receive state and federal funds. Many facilities accept payment from insurance programs (United Health Care, Humana, Kaiser, etc). Let's look at the different methods of paying for long-term care or nursing home stays.

Private Pay

Payment for nursing home care comes from personal funds if the nursing facility stay is not covered by other programs (Medicare, Medicaid, VA, etc.). The daily rate covers room and board, twenty-four-hour nursing care, three meals a day, utilities, activities, and some routine items, but may not include drugs ordered, certain supplies, and therapy. Daily rates are close to and above one hundred dollars a day. That's not too bad a deal considering all that's covered, but the cost of a nursing home stay from private funds can be quite costly over a long period of time. Most often residents will exhaust all their assets and will have to apply for Medicaid.

Medicaid

Medicaid is that public assistance once a person has spent down all his or her assets and no longer has the ability to pay for nursing home care. About 90 percent of nursing home facilities in Georgia are paid for by Medicaid. In order to be eligible for Medicaid, people must submit documents and applications showing that they no longer have funds to pay for their nursing home stay. Documents include bank statements, life and burial policies, mortgage documents, birth certificates, Social Security card, Medicare card, verification of income, etc. You may contact the facility's financial manager for details. You will be given the contact information for the person representing the local Department of Family and Children Services (DFACS). Medicaid eligibility depends upon a person's resources, income, and medical need. The exact amount of resources will vary from state to state.

Medicare Part A

Medicare part A, often called "major medical" or hospital insurance, pays for about 10 percent of nursing home stays. The resident must meet specific clinical and technical criteria in order to be eligible for Medicare A to pay for the first twenty days of coverage in a skilled nursing center. There are strict guidelines to be met to maintain compliance with Medicare coverage (daily skilled services). A person can be eligible for up to one hundred total days per spell of illness as long as criteria have been met. Some people purchase Medicare supplemental policies that may help pay all or a portion of the remaining eighty days of coinsurance payment as long as the person is still meeting the coverage criteria. Medicare co-insurance rate increases each year. When the services are no longer medically necessary or the person reaches goals to complete the daily skilled service, timely notices are given to the beneficiary or his or her designee. This gives the person the opportunity to appeal the decision of coverage ending.

Medicare Part B

Medicare part B coverage, referred to as "medical insurance," comes from additional premiums paid by the beneficiary. Medicare Part B only covers part of the qualified charges, which usually leaves 20 percent or more to be paid by the resident. Medicare Part B often pays for therapies, labs, ambulance, and other services.

Medicare Part D

Medicare Part D is the prescription drug coverage available to those covered by Medicare. Each state has prescription drug plans that are offered, regardless of a person's income.

Veterans Administration

Some nursing homes have contracts with the Veterans Administration that in turn provides care to residents under the VA benefits. Nursing homes receive daily rates from the VA that covers a resident's health care needs as well as room and board.

Private Health Insurance

Private insurance policies may not pay for any nursing home coverage, while others will pay for a certain amount of days or certain therapies and/or room and board. Nursing homes may choose to bill the resident, and then that person can file directly with the insurance for reimbursement.

Long-term Care Insurance

These policies can be varied, and the person obtaining the policy usually chooses the amounts of benefits paid by the day, inflation adjustments, waiting, and benefit periods. Be cautious in selecting your policy when determining the specific coverage for long-term care.

Ms. B. was visited by her pastor on Sunday afternoon. At the end of the visit, the pastor apologized for eating all of the peanuts she had in a bowl by her chair. She replied, "Well, that's all right. Since I lost my teeth, all I can do is suck the chocolate off of them!"

In selecting a nursing home, you'll find you are using all your senses. You should also go with that "sixth sense," or your gut instinct. You will find you may have doubts about the entire process, and once the final decision on a facility is made, you may still find that you second-guess yourself. You can use the points below that are divided by the senses to help in your selection of a facility.

Sense of smell:

- When you walk into the facility, do you smell any overwhelming and unpleasant odors? Naturally, as you tour a facility you will run across some odors that indicate normal bodily function. I need not tell you what those odors would be. These odors may be in spot areas of the facility but should not be throughout the facility. Notice any strong urine odors, especially if not really focused around the resident's rooms. Public restrooms should be clean and without unnecessary odors.
- If you are touring a facility during a mealtime, you may be able to notice the smells of the meals. Hopefully you won't be touring the day they are cooking salmon croquets or cabbage!

Sense of touch:

- What do the temperatures feel like throughout the facility? Older persons may be more cold-natured and prefer to have warmer rooms and other areas.
- Are the handrails in hallways firmly in place when you hold to them?
- Are the floors clean and free of stickiness or wetness?

Sense of sight:

- Look around as you enter the facility. Does the facility seem well lighted? Is the furniture sturdy and stable so as not to tip over? Is the facility clean, neat, and up to your standards of cleanliness and upkeep?
- As you tour the facility, look at the residents. Do they look well groomed, in appropriate seasonal clothing, positioned comfortably in chairs? Are residents restrained with trays over their chairs or belts tied across the front and then on the chair, etc.?
- Do the rooms have windows and privacy curtains? Is staff using the privacy curtains?
- Do the residents have dressers and closets to hold their clothes and personal items? Is the room big enough to allow access for ease in movement with either a walker or wheelchair?
- Do you see call lights on over the doors or hear alarms going off for long periods of time?
- What do you see regarding interactions between the staff and residents? Are staff members addressing the residents with respect and using the proper names? Are they courteous and friendly?
- Do you see calendars posted that reflect activities for the residents? Are the patients participating in activities?

Sense of hearing:

- What do you hear regarding staff interactions? Are they courteous and kind in how they communicate to the resident? Are they responding to calls for help?

- Do you hear call bells and other alarms going off without being answered in a timely manner?

Sense of taste:

- You should be allowed to try a sample of the meals prepared for the residents. There may be a small cost for this. Does the food look and smell appealing? Is the temperature adequate for the food item—cold foods cold, hot foods hot?

As I mentioned, you can use your "sixth sense" as well. Is this a place where you could leave your loved one and be able to sleep at night? Do you feel any uneasiness about placing your loved one in this facility? Plan your visits either in coordination with the admissions director for a guided tour, or you may visit the facility after normal business hours or on weekends. Most often, the staff can take you on tour any time you drop by. When you meet the facility representative, have some questions ready to ask. Here are some examples to help you get started.

- What types of payment does the facility accept? Are they certified to deliver services provided by Medicaid and Medicare?
- What services are covered in the daily rate? What specific services are not covered?
- Does the facility have emergency plans in place and coordinate with local hospitals in case of an evacuation or disaster?

- What is the staffing pattern? Are staffing numbers posted on a visible area? Is staff available to help with activities of daily living (ADLs)?
- Does the administrator have a current license with the state? Does the facility have a current license to operate?
- Are the most recent survey results posted?
- Ask the staff about the physician services. How often do they visit? Can a resident's own physician be assigned?
- How does the facility get in touch with the physician when there is an emergency?
- How are residents allowed to make decisions about their care? Are families and residents allowed to be part of the plan of care?
- What activities are offered? Are residents assisted to activities?
- What kinds of diets are offered? Are residents' likes and dislikes taken into consideration for meal planning? Does a registered dietitian plan the menus and specific diets?
- What happens if a resident is hungry in the middle of the night or after dining hours are closed? Are snacks available?
- Does the facility have a therapy department that offers physical, occupational, and speech therapy services? How does the facility maintain residents' current physical functioning and psychosocial well-being?
- Is there a social worker on staff?
- How are complaints and concerns handled? How does the staff handle issues of quality of care?

- Does the staff respect residents' wishes with regards to religious preferences? Are arrangements made that will allow residents to participate in worship of their choice?
- Do residents have access to money? Can they keep a small amount of funds for their personal use?
- Are beautician and/or barber services offered? What are the fees associated with the beauty shop, nail care, etc.?
- Are licensed nurses available twenty-four hours a day? Is there a medical director on staff?
- Does the facility have a pharmacist to review medications? Can residents use their own pharmacy to provide medications?
- Does the facility specialize in caring for those with dementia or Alzheimer's? Does the facility have a separate floor or unit to care for these types of residents?
- How does the facility ensure safety for those residents who may wander?
- Does the facility have written policies and procedures? Does the facility have a written Bill of Rights for the resident?
- Is staff trained in respecting residents' privacy and caring for them with dignity?
- Does the facility have a family council? Resident council? How often do they meet?

Residents have rights while living in a facility. Here are a few for examples:

- Residents have a right to be informed about their care and make decisions about their care.
- Residents have the right to vote, manage their own money, and participate in activities both inside and outside of the facility.
- Residents have the right to privacy and confidentiality. They can use a phone in private, receive mail unopened, and visit with family and friends in private. They have the right to consensual sexual activity. They have a right to privacy regarding their medical care and personal affairs.
- Residents have the right to be treated with respect and dignity, and to be cared for without physical threat or emotional or sexual injury or harm. They may not be restrained physically or chemically unless there is a reasonable need and with the physician's approval.
- Residents have the right to file a complaint to the state if there has been abuse or neglect of mismanagement of their personal funds. Residents cannot be discharged for filing grievances or raising concerns.

This is just a brief highlight of the many rights that residents have while living in a nursing home. The staff is frequently trained in residents' rights and the protection of residents. The Social Services department can offer assistance in handling residents' grievances and concerns.

It is very important that you do your research on facilities you may be considering for your loved one. Many times, due to an emergency need (for example, a fall with a fractured hip), there is not a lot of time to drive around and look for just the right one. All nursing homes in Georgia are inspected by state and federal survey teams at least once a year. Surveyors on this team are comprised of registered nurses, social workers, dietitians, and even pharmacists. Nursing homes must pass rigorous regulations set by the Centers for Medicaid and Medicare Services (CMS). There are over five hundred regulations that facilities must comply with on a regular basis. The long-term care profession is one of the most heavily regulated industries in the nation.

Don't wait until a loved one is in need of nursing home placement that may put you in a position to make a hasty decision. If you have an aging parent, grandparent, a sibling who may be ill, etc., start considering your options for what is available in your community. It could be an assisted living center or a nursing home. Nursing homes of today are not like they were even ten years ago. Many facilities offer specialized focus on rehabilitation, wound care, or dementia care. Facilities are constantly seeking new ways to meet the needs of their community and are making advances in quality of care by participating in several advancing excellence programs in coordination with their state nursing home associations and the American Health Care Association.

Having worked in the nursing home industry for over twenty years, I could not imagine a more rewarding job. In fact, I don't consider what I do each day a "job." I look forward to going to work. I enjoy seeing residents get better and go home or to other living options within their community. When circumstances do not allow the resident to leave, I can feel pleased in the fact that I have done the best I could do in meeting my residents' needs. I find a simple thank you or a hug around the neck is that little spark I need to keep going. Staff members who care for the residents in my facility, as in most facilities, really do love what they do and become attached to the residents. They genuinely try to do their best in providing the care our elderly population needs and more importantly deserves.

Here are some resources that may be helpful to you in your quest for finding a nursing home to meet the needs of your loved one.

Georgia Health Care Association (www.ghca.info)
678-289-6555

Georgia Dept. of Community Health—Medicaid
404-656-4507

Alzheimer's Association
800-272-3900

Centers for Medicare/Medicaid Services
877-267-2323

Social Security Administration
800-772-1213

Medicare
800-633-4227

Eldercare Locator
800-677-1116

Veteran's Affairs Regional Office
800-827-1000

American Health Care Association
202-842-4444

Links

- www.roadtorecovery.com

Guidance in Choosing a Nursing Home

- www.consumersresearch.cnc.org (Consumers Research Council of America)
- www.aplaceformom.com
- www.medicare.gov (Use this link for the nursing home compare section.)
- www.newlifestyles.com (senior resident care options)

Made in the USA
Charleston, SC
18 October 2016